The French Revolution. A Quick Immersion

Quick Immersions use accurate and straightforward language to offer a good introduction, or deeper knowledge, on diverse issues. Well structured texts by prestigious authors, they delve into the worlds of political and social science, philosophy, hard science and the humanities.

Jay M. Smith

THE FRENCH REVOLUTION
A Quick Immersion

Tibidabo Publishing
New York

Copyright © 2020 by Jay M. Smith

Published by Tibidabo Publishing, Inc. New York.

All rights reserved. No part of this publication may be reproduced, stored in a retrieval system, or transmitted, in any form or by any means, electronic, mechanical, photocopying, recording, scanning or otherwise, without the prior permission in writing with the Publisher or as permitted by law, or under terms agreed upon with the appropriate reprographics rights organization.

Copyediting by Lori Gerson
Cover art by Raimon Guirado
For illustration copyrights, please see page 7.

First published 2020

Visit our Series on our Web:
www.quickimmersions.com

Library of Congress Control Number: 2020940997

ISBN: 978-1-949845-14-3
1 2 3 4 5 6 7 8 9 10

Printed in the United States of America.

Contents

List of illustrations 7
Preface 9
1. Prelude to Crisis: 1771-1788 13
2. The Stakes of Conflict 34
3. Division and Mistrust in a World Remade 68
4. War and the Republican Turn 111
5. From Popular Purge to Armed Repression:
   Power to "the People" and Back Again 140
Further reading 184

List of illustrations

Chapter 1

1. Copy of the French silver coin minted in 1776 by Louis XVI. 17
© Gors4730/123RF.com

Chapter 2

2. Palace of Versailles, France. 51
© Felix Lipov /123RF.com

Chapter 3

3. Statue of Queen Marie-Antoinette in the basilica of Saint-Denis. 88
© Isogood/123RF.com

4. Motto "Liberté, Egalité, Fraternité", town hall of Paris, France. 105
© Johny007pan/123RF.com

5. Maximilien Robespierre. 108
© Ruslan Gilmanshin/123RF.com

Chapter 4

6. Louvre Palace. 127
© Vadim Moiseev /123RF.com

7. *Monument aux Girondins in Bordeaux*. France. 135
© WJarek/123RF.com

Chapter 5

8. Statue of Napoleon Bonaparte, Les Invalides, Paris, France. 175
© Oleksii/123RF.com

Preface

The French Revolution changed the world irrevocably. Its script provided the template for modern revolutions down through the twentieth century. Depending on how one defines the event, its many twists and turns spanned six years, a decade, or more than a quarter-century. The crises spurred by the Revolution launched military conflicts that left millions dead and changed the face of European warfare. The dramas of the Revolution called to the stage a cast of characters as colorful, eloquent, courageous and tragic as that from any episode in human history. How does the historian quickly immerse readers in such an event, one whose mysteries have elicited more than two hundred years of rich and conflicting expert analysis?

The French Revolution. A Quick Immersion does not aspire to provide a concise but serviceable "survey" of the French Revolution. To qualify as a genuine survey, the book would need to work in many neglected topics —the Festival of the Supreme Being, the Revolutionary calendar, and the making of the metric system do not even register in this account— and important individuals, including towering figures like Lafayette, would require more sustained attention. Instead of surveying the full terrain of the Revolution, readers of this book are prompted to reflect on several major themes that defined the Revolution's novelty, determined its inescapably contentious course, and shaped its legacy for later generations.

Although the book tells the story of "the French Revolution", the story's contours are largely determined by attention to prominent forces that made recurring impacts on the evolving project of the Revolution down to 1795. I want to suggest that the essence of the French Revolution can be reduced to four new challenges the French had to surmount after king Louis XVI made his momentous decision to seek the nation's help in addressing an unmanageable fiscal crisis: 1) the fraught effort to reconfigure the social order under the pressure of increasingly powerful ideas favoring equality; 2) the process of reinventing government in a context of incessant crisis; 3) the need to balance the power and prerogatives of the people, in whose name the

Revolution was made, against those of their leaders —whether anointed, self-appointed, or elected; 4) the difficulty of establishing trust and confidence between citizens navigating their way through the void created by a crumbling monarchy led by a dishonest king. I will argue that the intractability of these problems, including especially the widespread failure of trust, can be traced to a sequence of pivotal and high-stakes confrontations —many of them occurring even before the Revolution was fully in motion— that left festering doubts about the intentions and the reliability of key actors. This structuring theme of the French Revolution remained active until the Revolution began to reverse its course in 1794-1795, where this narrative ends.

One could make the case that other features of the revolutionary experience deserve equal weight in the telling of the story. Other accounts of the period between 1789 and 1799 have emphasized, for example, the state's use of organized political violence during and after the so-called Reign of Terror of 1793-1794; the role of religious ideas and practices in the structuring of both revolution and counter-revolution; the attempt to construct a unifying civic culture suffused by revolutionary values; the profound experiential differences that fell along lines of race, gender and class through the entire event of the Revolution; and the wide global dimensions of the ideological and political rupture that the Revolution immediately came to represent.

These and other subjects are all eminently worthy, but no short book can encompass all aspects of the French Revolution. Thankfully, some of these other important themes are at least glimpsed through the four analytical lenses that are given priority in this quick immersion, each of which seeks to bring into focus a capacious kind of political activity. In the process of working out the internal dynamics of their Revolution, readers shall see, the French reimagined the relationship of citizen to citizen; they established a template for democratic self-governance the influence of which is still felt today; they wrestled to define the social parameters and the inherent political rights of a newly empowered "public" previously conceived only in the abstract; they fought paradigmatic ideological battles whose echoes resounded for two centuries and more; and they internationalized liberation struggles and the warfare to which such struggles gave rise. For all these reasons, through their Revolution the French created the framework within which political practice and ideology, social movements, democratic culture, nationhood, patriotism and warfare have been performed and imagined across much of the world for the past two hundred years. An event of such magnitude invites sustained immersion and deep study. May this first taste of the French Revolution whet the reader's appetite for further exploration.

What moved the French to initiate their world-changing Revolution? This is the question taken up in chapter one.

Chapter 1
Prelude to Crisis: 1771-1788

When the people's elected representatives arrived at Versailles in May 1789 to convene the Estates-General of the realm —a kingdom-wide representative assembly that had last met in 1614— none of the deputies imagined that they were about to embark on a political experiment that would result in the abolition of nobility, the elimination of feudalism, the toppling of the monarchy, the beheading of a king and a queen, the liberation of slaves in the French Caribbean, a series of wars against virtually all the powers of Europe, and the crowning of an emperor (Napoleon, in 1804) who had earned renown as a general in those wars. All of this is simply to say that none of the representatives of the Three Estates of the realm was a clairvoyant in 1789. In their time as in ours, even the wisest political actors struggled to forecast the future.

It would be wrong to assume, however, that no one had premonitions of momentous change coming over the horizon. On the contrary, everyone who showed up for the opening ceremony of the Estates-General on May 5, 1789 knew that they were participating in an extraordinary political gathering —a gathering unprecedented in their own lifetimes— made necessary by a fiscal crisis of unmanageable scope. The solution to the crown's fiscal crisis, everyone understood, would necessarily entail fundamental changes in the way the government shared its powers, made its decisions, levied taxes, and borrowed money. Why would the deputies to the Estates-General have known all of this beforehand? They would have known it because the royal government had spent the previous two years desperately trying to implement fundamental reforms of its own. Having been blocked at every turn, the monarchy summoned the Estates-General in a final cry for help. This dramatic capitulation, announced in July 1788, plainly portended a dramatic revision of a political system that had come to be defined by its dysfunctionality.

The basic sources of the dysfunction have been described often and were widely recognized at the time. French society was organized in a hierarchy of three Estates, with the First Estate (the clergy) and the Second Estate (the nobility) enjoying legal, cultural, and fiscal advantages that the commoners of the Third Estate were generally denied. Although they amounted to no more than about three percent of the population, the first two Estates, allowing for considerable regional variations, owned somewhere between fifteen and forty percent of the land. The owners of these lands paid none of the basic land tax, the *taille*, owed by peasants and other commoners, and they enjoyed other fiscal exemptions as well. Privileges, including some that belonged to favored members of the Third Estate, had proliferated in the course of the eighteenth century, as the state found in the distribution of saleable privileges a useful tool of indirect fiscal extraction and a means of purchasing acquiescence in the political status quo among the elites. Privilege therefore became, simultaneously, more sought after and more resented by those disadvantaged by them.

The prospect of correcting for inequities, and of creating more efficient and productive revenue streams for the state, remained consistently bleak for two reasons. First, because of the ways in which monarchical power had been consolidated in the seventeenth century, kings had no interest in sharing power with a representative and deliberative body that might seek meaningful changes in the operations of the state. Second, factionalism at the royal court and noble intransigence in certain law courts on which the monarchy relied to affirm its laws consistently impeded or undermined reformist ideas that would threaten privileges to which various constituencies were attached. The last decades of the pre-Revolutionary era, though marked by intellectual dynamism and the broad cultural efflorescence known by the name of Enlightenment, had seen a repetitive cycle of ambitious fiscal and economic reform followed by dissent or unrest and capped inevitably by reversal.

One Step Forward, Two Steps Back

On August 20, 1786, the controller-general Charles-Alexandre de Calonne made a sobering announcement to Louis XVI (r. 1774-1792). He informed the king that more than half of his annual revenues were being used to pay interest on the debt, and that bankruptcy could no longer be staved off without radical reforms. Although the severity of the immediate crisis may have surprised the king, the need for reform would not have come as a shock. Ever since the Seven Years' War (1756-1763), the French crown had been experimenting with various fiscal expedients to help meet its financial obligations. By design, the French political system lacked a national representative assembly, on the model of English parliament, that could be expected to approve new taxes and loans on a regular basis. Royal ministers therefore resorted to short-term fixes. The controversial character of most of those measures had led to protracted disputes between the agents of the crown and the preeminent judicial bodies —called *parlements*— of the realm. The noble magistrates in the thirteen *parlements*, charged with the responsibility of registering all new laws and safeguarding the principles of France's traditional and unwritten constitution, had come to regard themselves as proxy spokesmen for the "nation", and as defenders of its rights and liberties. After about 1750 they even regularly published their objections to proposed legislation, thereby inviting the growing French reading public to reflect on the constitutional issues in play whenever the *parlements* chose to push back against the authority of the king.

1. Copy of the French silver coin minted in 1776 by Louis XVI.

So obstructionist did the *parlements* become over the course of the 1760s that king Louis XV and his chancellor, René Nicolas de Maupeou, subjected them to a radical reorganization in 1771. They carried out what was called at the time a "revolution" against the courts. The venerable *parlement* of Paris, the most important court in the country, with a tradition that stretched back to the thirteenth century, was simply dissolved and reconstituted with many of its powers shorn away and with new, more pliant, officers registering royal laws with minimal complaint. The magistrates of the former *parlements* had owned their offices as property —a structural condition, inherited from the sixteenth century, that made them immune to removal. No more. Maupeou ended "venality of office" for judgeships and made the new magistrates salaried employees of the crown. He imposed equally dramatic changes on virtually all of the provincial *parlements*. In the short term Maupeou's coup did ameliorate the condition of crown finances. Maupeou's client and partner, the controller-general Joseph-Marie Terray, pushed through new tax assessment procedures that ensured a more even and thorough allotment of the tax burden, he introduced a new tax on the remaining venal offices in the realm, and the hated universal tax known as the twentieth tax (on annual income), which had occasioned almost non-stop conflict with the *parlements* since its invention in 1749, was finally rendered permanent by the courts in 1771. By 1772, the budget was nearly in balance.

Maupeou and Terray, however, were unable to build on these first steps. The Maupeou revolution inspired impassioned protest on the part of a self-styled "patriot party" that opposed political tactics it deemed both unconstitutional and despotic. This party, consisting of former magistrates, lawyers, disaffected grandees and the writers they subsidized, launched a withering but underground propaganda campaign against the chancellor. Wishing to strike a conciliatory chord at the outset of his own reign in 1774, Louis XVI dismissed Maupeou, recalled the former *parlements*, and restored the venal status of the magistrates' offices. Thus began a fifteen-year history of royal vacillation and fitful, usually abortive, efforts to put the royal finances on a firmer and more rational footing.

The two men who succeeded Terray at the head of crown finances, first Anne-Robert-Jacques Turgot and then Jacques Necker, both came from the world of the Enlightenment. Turgot was associated with the visionary school of economists known as the "physiocrats;" Necker's wife hosted one of Paris's most popular salons in the 1770s and 1780s, where the couple socialized with luminaries such as Buffon, Grimm, and Diderot. Both men brought to their positions a reformist zeal worthy of the boldest philosophes. Between 1774 and 1776 Turgot attempted to liberalize the economy by suppressing certain monopolies, lifting regulations on the grain trade, and boosting productivity by eliminating landowners' feudal right (the *corvée*) over a portion of their peasants' labor. Predictably, the beneficiaries of the privileges he sought to eliminate complained bitterly of Turgot's high-handedness. Nor did ordinary people prove more receptive to the controller-general's experiment with laissez-faire principles. After the price of bread surged following the freeing of the grain trade in 1774, rioters took to the streets across northern France in spring 1775; the uprisings were so numerous and dangerous that contemporaries referred to them collectively as the "flour war". Louis XVI, always vulnerable to the whispering campaigns pushed by his courtiers, some of whom had developed a strong dislike for Turgot, dismissed the controller-general in May 1776. His reforms were undone.

In the short run, Jacques Necker fared little better. Having made a splash in the world of letters by writing an *Essay on legislation and the grain trade* quite critical of Turgot's hands-off policy with respect to grain prices, Necker was invited to serve as director-general of the royal treasury in 1776. (A Protestant banker from Geneva, Necker's religious identity made him ineligible to sit on the king's council, thus barring him technically from the controller-general position). Despite facing the burden of having to manage France's financial assistance for the American War of Independence that Louis XVI decided to support in 1777, Necker, like his predecessor Turgot, was a man of ideas determined to try out new strategies for bolstering the king's credit and inspiring confidence in royal policy.

He conspicuously slashed expenses, sharply reducing the size of the royal household, while simultaneously raising little in the way of new taxes. He sought to create a sense of real participation in the government's business by creating two experimental provincial assemblies, in Berry and Haute-Guyenne, that allowed a cross-section of provincial notables to have a hand in tax apportionment and the direction of public works projects. He also sought to professionalize the state's financial bureaucracy by cutting away at a bloated corps of venal officeholders and replacing them with a leaner staff of salaried experts who were both more capable and less entitled.

Most notably, perhaps, Necker used the new force of publicity to rally support for the government and to forge a more open and ostensibly dialogical relationship between rulers and ruled. His efforts along these lines reflected his deep familiarity with international finance and the mechanisms of credit, where the faith and confidence of lenders counted for everything. They also grew from his acute awareness of the burgeoning published literature of the Enlightenment and of the ways in which that literature had shaped and reshaped public opinion since mid-century.

The Power of Publicity

In 1781 Necker took the unprecedented step of publishing a detailed account of the king's annual budget, explaining in a long preamble addressed to the king the salutary effects he expected both the monarch and the people to derive from this gesture toward transparency. Rendering public the details of the budget would prove "infinitely useful" to the king, he wrote, because it would set a precedent of openness and forthrightness that all royal servants would be obliged to follow thereafter. Pointing to the future, Necker noted, "the obligation to place in broad daylight all the work of his administration would influence the very first steps taken by a Minister of Finances in the career he must pursue". "Publicity" would promise future ministers the recompense of honor —awarded through public approbation— if only they remained aware "of the importance of [their] duties and the necessity of fulfilling them". The benefits of publicity would be reciprocal, since the king's subjects, feeling informed and included, would respond with patriotic appreciation toward the king and his government. Public opinion "grants the nation a sort of influence", and a wise king must learn to appeal to this new force. The king's power ultimately rested on "confidence…this union of opinions, this spirit of society, this continual communication between [citizens]". Louis XVI's recourse to publicity would provide an indirect means for gaining the consent of the governed.

Necker's *Account for the King* was published in February 1781. Within three months the director-general had vacated his office, having failed to retain the confidence of Louis XVI. Already in the late 1770s, Necker's abolition of lucrative offices in the royal treasury, and his economizing measures at court, had stirred resentment in the entourage surrounding the king. The publication of the budget in 1781 further aggravated tensions because Necker had displayed for all to see the true costs of the pensions lavished on court favorites and members of the royal family. Without drawing explicit conclusions for his readers, he juxtaposed the generous financial benefits enjoyed by the privileged with the strain placed on the royal coffers. His critics, who included the brother of the king and other ministers who had grown tired of Necker's austerity program, immediately launched a campaign to discredit his numbers and his character. This campaign, like the anti-Turgot campaign of 1776, quickly hit its mark.

Louis XVI's weak will and the concerted efforts of courtiers who resented Necker's power and wide popularity certainly help to explain the Genevan's sudden fall from grace. This climax to his innovative reforming career —or first career, since he would return to power in the crisis conditions of 1788— also needs to be seen, however, in light of the fundamental conflict that culminated in the publication of the *Account for the King*. This conflict lay at the heart of all the failed reform efforts that marked the last two decades of the "*Ancien Régime*", as the French would later call the period before the Revolution.

Simply put, the changes that Necker sought to implement eroded both the regime of privilege that had long defined the French social order and the core political assumptions underlying monarchical absolutism. In subtle but important ways, he proposed to empower and enable the common mass of citizens —the Third Estate. The provincial assemblies he piloted in Berry and Haute-Guyenne, which he had hoped would serve as models for the entire realm, gave commoners as many seats as those held by the clergy and the nobility, who were accustomed to exercising outsize influence in local affairs. His abolition of venal offices (sounding echoes of Maupeou's coup) suggested that the cause of reform would require at least some aristocrats to surrender standing, property, and some of their legal privileges, even though they regarded themselves as the king's preeminent servants. Most dramatically, the *Account for the King*, in sharing with the reading public how much revenue the king collected and how he chose to use that revenue, subtly undermined the assumption that the king was accountable to no one but God. The notion that all political authority rested in the king's hands had been a bedrock principle of absolutist governance since the aftermath of the Wars of Religion (1562-1598) and the age of Richelieu.

In a critical assessment of Necker's *Account for the King* written soon after its release, an anonymous magistrate reflected the still-prevailing wisdom in the circles of government. "If secrecy is the soul of the affairs of individuals, secrecy regarding the state of a state is even more so". For any minister, then, "it is essential to conform to the constant practice of the monarchy, and not show the state of the finances to anyone except the king and his council". Only in unusual circumstances should details of the royal accounts be shared with anyone else, and then "only to persons of the most eminent rank". Necker's decision to disclose the inner workings of royal finance on an indiscriminate basis —to all who could read or listen patiently as the details were read to them— was widely regarded as a threat to the king's authority and to the status hierarchies with which it was associated. In Necker's recognition of an "obligation to place in broad daylight" the work of the government, and in his suggestion that an undifferentiated and anonymous public had a right to assess the government's work, the anonymous magistrate believed he detected a hidden motive: "to establish republican equality in France".

Despite his roots in the "republic" of Geneva, Necker had great respect for the institution of monarchy. And his support for the stabilizing benefits of status hierarchies led him to criticize the revolutionaries who would later go on to abolish nobility in 1790. The furor over the *Account for the King*, which became a bestseller, nevertheless shows the nature of the sensitivities with which reformers had to contend in the decades before the Estates-General of 1789. Maupeou, Turgot, and Necker each in his own way had taken measures to weaken or circumvent the sclerotic apparatus of privilege that inhibited both economic activity and the creation of an equitable system of taxation. In doing so they aroused the passionate opposition of corporate groups —the *parlements*, the guilds, the defenders of the traditional prerogatives of the nobility— who moved to protect their privileges both for self-interested reasons and because many believed that privilege provided an efficacious constitutional check on arbitrary executive power. Necker and Turgot, the latter also a champion of local representative assemblies, further sought to increase and improve public participation in the affairs of the state. Necker strongly hinted that the agents of the crown, if not the king himself, were accountable to a critical public capable of receiving and processing information about the state —or at least its fiscal operations. In the eyes of many, Necker put both the theory and practice of royal absolutism at risk.

So swift was the response to Necker's final gambit, and so emphatic the return to the status quo ante after his effective dismissal, that "reform" was put on hold for another five years. Necker's successors, first the *parlementaire* Jean-François Joly de Fleury and then, in 1783, Calonne, returned to the traditional crown practice of borrowing at high rates of interest in order to fund the state's operations and to meet a debt burden that had only grown worse thanks to the American war. Even the spigot of royal largess at court was reopened, with queen Marie-Antoinette and several of her confidantes, most notably the duchesse de Polignac, acquiring reputations for profligacy that would later come back to haunt them.

Running out of Options

When Calonne recognized in August 1786 that the inevitable could no longer be delayed, and that the state had to go all in on sweeping fiscal reforms or declare a bankruptcy that would leave the government inoperable, he himself gave expression to a sense of *déjà vu* that had to have been widely shared. He had drafted a reform package that won the approval of the king, and for which he now hoped to win broad public support (or at least the illusion of such support). His plans, he noted in February 1787, could hardly be regarded as "novelties". On the contrary. "They represent a summary of . . . the plans for the public good long contemplated by experienced statesmen and by the government itself. Some have been attempted in part and all seem to have the backing of the nation, but hitherto their complete implementation appeared impracticable" because of "conflicting interests" that had proved irreconcilable. Indeed, Calonne's reform plan contained many familiar items. He proposed the establishment of a series of deliberative assemblies, from parish to province, to enable "the expression of the taxpayers' wishes and their observations on everything which concerns them". (Crucially, representation would be determined by wealth and property, not by the estate to which one belonged). He announced, again, the freeing of the grain trade and the abolition of the *corvée*. A fairer tax system would be provided by a universal land tax from which no one would be exempt. Internal customs duties would be reduced and standardized to encourage economic activity. The self-evident rationality of these reforms, Calonne assumed, would also inspire the confidence the crown now needed to borrow money at low rates of interest.

Fully aware that the "conflicting interests" that had blocked or undone previous reform efforts remained powerful, Calonne chose a risky method of winning support for his do-or-die scheme. Knowing from recent experience that the noble magistrates of the *parlements* would likely object to the elimination of existing privileges and the disregard for estate in the composition of the proposed deliberative assemblies, he advised the king to convene an Assembly of Notables and to ask for the Assembly's endorsement of the plan. This idea was itself a sign of desperation, since no Assembly of Notables had been convened in France since 1626 and precedent provided no way of predicting delegates' response to the proposed reforms. Calonne seems mainly to have assumed that the key to success was to limit the number of magistrates as participants in the Assembly. Of the 144 delegates invited to Versailles for the meeting, only thirty-six were officers from the *parlements* and other "sovereign courts" (the *Chambres des Comptes*, the *Cours des Aides*, the *Cours des Monnaies*). If he succeeded in sidelining the judges from the *parlements*, however, Calonne miscalculated by making the voice of commoners (who had the most to gain from his reforms) essentially non-existent. Only a handful of his notables, hailing from cities across the realm, lacked noble status. The Notables politely reviewed Calonne's proposals, but in the end they rejected them. Calonne, who was now also publicly accused of engaging in improper speculation on the Parisian stock market, resigned in disgrace. The Notables had claimed, among other things, that their Assembly lacked the authority to approve new taxes. They urged the king, and the new controller-general Loménie de Brienne (ironically, a vocal opponent of Calonne's in the Assembly of Notables), to summon an Estates-General.

Not ready for such a drastic step, but worried by a fiscal crunch that was worsening by the day, Brienne went to the *parlement* of Paris, hoping against hope that the magistrates could be persuaded to accept a modified version of the reforms recently rejected by the Assembly of Notables. The judges made a few concessions, but Louis XVI's heavy-handed and unexpected attempt to force their acceptance of several emergency loans in November 1787 backfired spectacularly; after a heated confrontation during which the king aggressively asserted his absolute authority —he said of the loan legislation that "it is legal because it is my will"— the magistrates of the *parlement* became recalcitrant and remained so until the spring of 1788. They joined in calls for an Estates-General.

The political dynamic at work would have struck everyone as distressingly familiar. But in May 1788 the unfolding of events came to resemble —to use a perfectly apt anachronism— a bad movie sequel. (Or, in Marx's formulation, this was tragedy turning into farce). In a series of edicts, Brienne and Louis XVI offered a replay of the Maupeou revolution. The *parlements* were reorganized, the courts ceding much of their power to a new Plenary Court to be staffed in part by the king's own ministers. The magistrates, meanwhile, were placed on indefinite vacation. As if on cue, the remnants of the "patriot party" that had opposed Maupeou in the 1770s quickly joined the fray, recycling the constitutionalist rhetoric of the earlier battle and leading a pamphlet war against Brienne's "ministerial despotism". The outcry poured over into the streets, as protesters rioted in many cities and sought to block the judicial registration of the edicts that would have mothballed the provincial *parlements*. Ominously, popular unrest was merging with a noble and *parlementaire* resistance to the top-down institutional tinkering in which king and ministers had been engaged since late 1786.

As Necker looked on from the sidelines, Brienne spent the spring and summer of 1788 providing an object lesson in the importance of maintaining "confidence" in the management of the state. The May edicts had created a sense of chaos across the country, and Brienne's desperate efforts to shore up support for his program —he announced on 5 July that an Estates-General would meet soon, and he simultaneously invited all of the crown's subjects to share their opinions in writing about the form and procedures of the coming Estates meeting— only reinforced the atmosphere of uncertainty. Consequently, the state's credit collapsed in August. Literally unable to pay his debts, the king once again had to dismiss an unpopular and failed minister. Also for the second time during his reign, in September 1788 he restored the *parlements* to their full powers. He did this, however, not before reliving one other event from his earlier and more auspicious years on the throne. In late August he reappointed Jacques Necker as Director-General of Finances.

Because of the strength of his own personal credit, his embeddedness in an international banking network, and his popular reputation as a public-minded reformer, the reinstallation of Necker promised a return to normalcy, or at least to solvency. (And indeed, credit markets calmed immediately after his reappointment). But the sudden resuscitation of the Genevan's political career in France symbolized much more than the monarchy's craving for familiarity and stability in the late summer of 1788. His return amounted to an admission of defeat for the decades-long project of ministerial reform. Even more, his resurgence made clear the terms of that defeat. The cause of reform had crashed on the shoals of intransigence —both the absolutist intransigence of a monarchy still reluctant to share power and the elitist intransigence of an aristocracy unwilling to imagine a world in which inherited social status had no direct correlation with political and fiscal power. A restless populace, increasingly aroused to attention, looked on helplessly as the dueling intransigents fought to yet another stalemate.

The unique value of Jacques Necker in August 1788 lay in his ability to rally the opinions of a large and anonymous public, one that had no means of exerting formal influence in the existing political system. He reassured that public, by his mere presence, that structural changes involving the meaningful redistribution of authority were indeed imminent. The king, jealous of his own power, had no interest in delivering such a message. The nobility, and the institutions in which it was enmeshed, was fearful of such changes and bound to resist all except those that tilted the balance of power in its favor and away from royal ministers. Necker's presence communicated the possibility of an alternative path, one shaped by a sensitivity to public opinion and to the interests of a socially variegated political community that existed outside the world of the royal court and its august judicial institutions. The direction of that alternative path remained sufficiently murky to allow all parties to imagine a settlement advantageous to their interests, but the reappearance of Necker in August 1788 heralded the emergence of the "public" as an independent agent in France's worsening political and fiscal crisis. The fact that Necker immediately announced that the Estates-General would meet as early as January 1, 1789 —this time-table turned out to be overly optimistic— was no coincidence. In the popular imagination, Necker stood for the intervention of the public, and of an organ that could at last articulate compelling common interests, into a political impasse whose principal participants had been stuck on replay since the 1770s. The events of late 1788 and early 1789 would show that the symbolic triumph of the French public, and of the Third Estate with which it was implicitly associated, could not be overturned.

Chapter 2
The Stakes of Conflict

The political respite provided by Necker's return proved brief. For a month or so the nation looked forward with optimism toward the coming Estates-General meeting. The signs of renewed political engagement were unmistakable. In anticipation of the national meeting, many provinces carried out new experiments in political representation. Brienne had seen to the establishment of many of Calonne's parish and provincial assemblies in the summer and fall of 1787, and these assemblies operated on the basis of equal representation for the commoners and for the privileged orders and with voting by head rather than by order. Such voting procedures foreclosed the possibility that decisions could be held hostage by the obstinacy of the clergy or the nobility. Meanwhile, provinces where traditional "Estates-General" assemblies had fallen into disuse were now permitted to revive them. And these, too, generally adopted more deliberately inclusive electoral and internal voting schemes. The province of Dauphiné developed a particularly influential model. An *ad hoc* gathering at the town of Vizille agreed that at future provincial estates meetings, all delegates should be elected (that is, there would be no co-opting of members by provincial dignitaries or agents of the crown), the Third Estate would have as many delegates as the privileged orders, and all voting would be by head. Because the leaders of this Dauphiné movement, including Antoine Barnave and Jean-Joseph Mounier, would go on to play leading roles in the national Estates-General in 1789, the principles of Vizille informed deliberations in that larger assembly.

This loosening of political convention fit the atmosphere of the moment, in which the prospect of wider inclusion in the political process and good faith cooperation across the boundaries of estate suggested the possibility of a happy resolution to the fiscal crisis. The roots of that crisis lay, at least in part, in an encrusted social order defined by the jealous defense of privilege and a closed political system that allowed little ventilation from the outside. Yet here, in Dauphiné and other provinces, were new signs of openness and adaptability.

A moment of Truth

The political climate changed abruptly in late September. Soon after resuming its judicial functions, the *parlement* of Paris issued its own opinion about the procedures that should govern the Estates-General meeting. In an announcement that quickly altered the public image of the court, the magistrates declared on September 25 that the Estates-General should meet "according to the forms of 1614". This meant that each of the three Estates would have its own chamber with the same number of deputies, and that each chamber would have its own vote on all substantive matters. There are reasons to think that a prime motive for this peremptory announcement was to block the manipulation of the Estates's organization by Necker or other royal ministers. After all, Turgot, Necker, and Calonne had all shown a recent willingness to devise new blueprints for assembly organization that undercut certain noble privileges and seemed designed to produce outcomes desired by the crown. And Brienne's July invitation to all royal subjects to submit their own written proposals regarding the form and procedures of the Estates had been issued while the chief minister was simultaneously taking a wrecking ball to the crown's traditional justice system. The just back-from-the-dead *parlementaires*, no doubt having become more conscious of their identities as noblemen, had good reasons to be wary of the intentions of the crown.

Whatever their internal political calculations, however, the magistrates of the *parlement* had badly misjudged the likely public response to the declaration of September 25. Advocates for the Third Estate —the Estate that would now be entitled to one vote out of three in the coming assembly, despite making up ninety-seven percent of the population— saw the declaration as an insult. The magistrates' decision to opt for the "forms of 1614" not only ignored the dramatic transformations in the social and intellectual life of the realm that had taken place since the early seventeenth century —when witches were still being burned at the stake, when fewer than a quarter of the king's subjects were literate, and when France had not a single café (Paris alone had thousands by the 1780s). The magistrates' rigid adherence to the society of orders also ignored recent developments.

In his influential *Considerations on the Ancient and Present Form of French Government*, published posthumously in 1764, the one-time royal minister René-Louis d'Argenson had championed what he called a "popular government" built on a network of consultative bodies "in which all the people have an equal part, without regard to the distinction between nobles and commoners". Striking a similar chord, one year later the baron d'Holbach could be heard complaining, in an essay on "representatives" written for Denis Diderot's *Encyclopedia*, that representative institutions of the "feudal" era (i. e., the Estates-

General in France) had always failed to give voice to the "people, composed of farmers, inhabitants of the city and the countryside, manufacturers, in a word, the most numerous, the most laborious, the most useful part of society". Many physiocratic thinkers had likewise proposed representative assemblies that ignored distinctions of estate and focused on subjects' relationship to the means of production. In any case, since the 1760s aristocrats and educated members of the Third Estate had grown accustomed to speaking a common language of patriotism. They read and wept over the same sentimental novels. They attended the same plays. In Masonic lodges, which had grown in number and influence throughout the eighteenth century, they were united by fraternal bonds of friendship. All across the social spectrum, the subjects of Louis XVI had come to regard France not only as a kingdom but also as a "nation", and they increasingly referred to themselves not only as subjects but also as "citizens". As Alexis de Tocqueville indicated in his classic *The Old Regime and the French Revolution* (1856), France's political culture had grown increasingly homogeneous, rendering the boundaries of estate simultaneously more visible and more dubious.

Meanwhile, all recent developments in the political arena had pointed in the direction of a more genuinely representative organization for France's reborn representative assemblies. In 1781 Necker had hailed the rise of public opinion and the way in which it conferred "a certain influence" on the nation as a whole. The Assembly of Notables, in 1787, had resisted Calonne's provincial assemblies because they did away with the three Estates altogether. But in debating alternative models for those assemblies, the Notables agreed that it made sense for the provincial assemblies to proceed on the basis of voting by head. And five of the Notables' seven deliberative committees called for the Third Estate to have half *or more* of the seats in each assembly. Still more recently, Brienne's call for input into the design of the Estates-General in July 1788 had opened discussion about voting, law-making, and representation to all interested parties in the realm, and relaxation of censorship rules had democratized political discourse to a degree unprecedented in French national life.

In its decree of September 25 the *parlement* of Paris simply disregarded or knowingly rejected what had seemed to be a growing consensus around the need for more robust representation of the voices and perspectives of commoners in France's political system. They chose the most restrictive and tradition-bound model of representation available, one that left the Third Estate disempowered and the privileged orders poised to dictate the terms of fiscal and political reform. Even the royal government reinforced this reading of the September 25 decree. Hoping to turn the public at large against the obstructive *parlementary* "aristocracy" that had blocked its every effort at reform, the government sponsored political pamphlets that excoriated the *parlement* for selfishly defending privilege at the expense of the interests of the nation as a whole.

The Fracturing of the Anti-ministerial Party

The stakes of the developing national debate had suddenly come into sharp focus. Either the Estates-General would further entrench the rights and privileges of the first two orders of the realm or it would announce a new order of things in which the interests of the Third Estate would be accorded an influence consistent with its size, weight, and importance in French society. The roots of the dynamic that propelled the French Revolution through its first year can be traced to this moment in 1788. One of the great issues that pulsed through the entire Revolution had now been formally joined. To what extent should Louis XVI's subjects regard one another as equals? And what legal and political adjustments should be made to reflect the real social and cultural leveling the French had experienced since the middle of the eighteenth century?

With a provocative *parlementary* declaration focusing the attention of all the king's politically informed subjects, in the fall of 1788 France saw its first concerted national effort to sway public opinion in the direction of a particular political outcome:

the defeat of a retrograde aristocracy seeking to secure its privileged position in a shifting political landscape. Ironically, a cadre of nobles who shared the "patriot" political inclinations of all who had recently rallied against ministerial despotism took the lead in promoting a propaganda campaign that advanced the cause of the Third Estate throughout the fall and into the winter of 1789. Operating in an informal club that came to be called the "Society of Thirty", these nobles, joined by a handful of men of letters from the First and Third Estates, wrote or subsidized the writing and distribution of dozens if not hundreds of pamphlets that laid out the historical, philosophical, and political foundations for a different kind of Estates-General, one that would be broadly representative and would share actively in the making of law. There were differences of emphasis in these pamphlets, with some drawing from Jean-Jacques Rousseau's concept of the "general will" and others more clearly rooted in the recent battles against ministerial despotism, but one issue consistently emerged as the most pressing: the need to double the number of Third Estate delegates in the upcoming Estates-General.

The most influential of all the pamphlets published between the *parlement*'s September 25 decree and the opening of the Estates-General in May 1789, a pamphlet that may or may not have been sponsored by the Society of Thirty, was the *abbé* Joseph-Emmanuel Sieyès's *What is the Third Estate?*

Like all of the writers associated with the Society, the *abbé* formally advocated for the doubling of the Third Estate in the coming assembly. But in a brilliant rhetorical pirouette, Sieyès ultimately turned away from that "modest aim" by suggesting a much more ambitious political program that superseded the question of how many deputies should be convened in 1789.

That more ambitious program, filled out in one of the final chapters of his pamphlet, was in fact implicit on Sieyès's very first page. The *abbé*'s answer to the question that framed his pamphlet —what is the Third Estate?— was an emphatic EVERYTHING. He made clear from the opening that the Third Estate constituted a nation unto itself. Its activities drove the economy, produced all the items that circulated through the economy, and provided the services that allowed society to function. The Third Estate also possessed all the attributes —vigor, intelligence, education, courage, piety— thought necessary for the exercise of public functions. In fact, commoners already filled "nineteen-twentieths" of the positions in law, the army, the church, and administration, leaving only "the well paid and honorific posts" to be filled by "members of the privileged order". The Third Estate, Sieyès argued forcefully from his opening paragraphs, made up a self-sufficient nation by itself —with nation here being defined as "a body of associates living under *common* laws and represented by the same *legislative assembly*".

Developing his argument on these basic premises, to wit, that the Third Estate was a self-sufficient nation and that the members of any nation had to adhere to a common set of laws, Sieyès eventually dismissed the campaign for the doubling of the Third as "timid" and wrong-headed. If one "relies on true principle", Sieyès intoned, one is drawn ineluctably to the conclusion that the deputies of the three Estates "cannot vote *together* at all, either by heads or by orders". Dedicated to different interests because they were subject to different legal regimes —one for the privileged and one for everybody else— France's three orders could not forge a common and collective interest at all. Each order, in effect, constituted a separate nation, "no more competent to interfere in the affairs of the other orders than the States-General of Holland or the Council of Venice are to vote in the debates of the English Parliament". Even a thinker as astute as Sieyès could not see the future, but he called on the Third Estate to put aside the debate over the procedures of the Estates-General and to declare its own chamber a "National Assembly", arrogating to itself the power to provide the nation a proper constitution. Some six months later, in June 1789, the deputies of the Third Estate would do just that, seeming to validate the *abbé*'s predictive powers.

Before that important event could come to pass, however, a whole cascade of other conflicts and debates, all with uncertain outcomes, would first need to create the circumstances wherein the Third

Estate's self-anointment as a National Assembly could seem both plausible and desirable to large numbers of elected deputies. In January 1789, when Sieyès published his pamphlet, the political atmosphere was still confused and uncertain. With his pamphlet, however, Sieyès focused and simplified the Third Estate's task, and he suggested a clear way forward. The threat of ministerial despotism now seemed beside the point. The First Estate, to which Sieyès belonged, barely registered in the pamphlet's catalog of grievances. The unpopular Austrian queen was never mentioned, nor was the Paris *parlement* singled out for criticism. Sieyès pointed the finger at one enemy alone: the nobility.

Sieyès made the category of nobility the receptacle for all the sordid "abuses" for which the current regime had come to be known. Using rhetorical sleight of hand, he labeled the nobility "the privileged order", even though subjects of all three Estates in fact enjoyed legal privileges. He made this "privileged order" responsible for an entire system of governance that left commoners always disadvantaged. Manipulating their social connections, leveraging their wealth, and propagating the myth of their superiority, members of the privileged order had seized all positions of power and influence. They constituted a "vast aristocracy which overruns every part of France" and, for all intents and purposes, ruled in the king's name. "The usurpation is total; in every sense of the word, they reign". By contrast, "in France a man who is protected only by the common laws is a nobody; whoever is totally unprivileged must submit to every form of contempt, insult and humiliation".

The unjust character of the French social and political order could not have been rendered in starker terms. The Third Estate, even with all the skills, talents, and numbers sufficient to form a nation, instead had to endure the "contempt" of a tiny and self-satisfied minority who, like parasites, were best regarded as "foreign" to the true national body. By reformulating in this manner the ongoing conflict over the forms of the Estates-General, Sieyès infused righteous anger into a debate often weighed down by technical discussions of historical precedent and the putative spirit of an unwritten constitution. His rhetoric galvanized readers and defined the target of their rage. Nobles, by Sieyès's logic, would need to surrender their privileges before gaining admission to a reconstituted French nation.

Toward the Estates-General

Only days before the publication of *What is the Third Estate?*, the royal government made an announcement that would defer indefinitely full consideration of Sieyès's arguments. On December 27, 1788, Necker issued a "Result of the Royal Council" specifying that the upcoming Estates-General meeting would have as many representatives from the Third Estate as from the other two Estates combined. After having consulted with the reconvened Assembly of Notables, which mounted a conservative argument in favor of the forms of 1614, and after convening with individual members of the Paris *parlement*, who expressed support for increasing commoners' representation (so long as vote by order was retained), Necker indeed doubled the Third. The minister declined to give instructions on voting procedures, leaving a critical issue unresolved and promising further confusion in the months to come. But the doubling of the Third was a welcome symbolic concession to the advocates of the Third Estate —Parisians lit bonfires in celebration— and, just as important, it officially affirmed that the Estates-General would indeed be an assembly of Estates *qua* separate Estates.

In late January the election process began. The Estates-General would have about 1,200 delegates, apportioned according to each administrative district's population and tax contributions. All males at least twenty-five years of age and inscribed on local tax rolls were allowed to participate in the election of representatives. For commoners, the process unfolded in two stages, with parish-level electors being sent on to a district-level election that virtually assured that only men of means and education would gain election and be sent to Versailles. Elections for the first two estates were more direct and democratic. In the end, the First Estate elected simple parish priests in large numbers, military officers and distinguished lineages were over-represented in the delegation of the Second Estate, and the Third Estate chose lawyers or officials with legal training to voice its collective will.

The electoral assemblies established in the winter of 1789 had one other key responsibility assigned to them. Perhaps in an effort to scrupulously follow the precedent of 1614, the king asked all electoral assemblies to draft grievance lists (*cahiers de doléances*) that could inform the work of the Estates-General and communicate the people's will directly to the king. The process produced some 40,000 lists in total, at the parish and district levels. The subject of a rigorous quantitative and qualitative analysis carried out by sociologists John Markoff and Gilbert Shapiro over the course of the 1980s and 1990s, the grievance lists provide an intriguing snapshot of French public opinion on the eve of the greatest political and social upheaval the world had ever seen.

The *cahiers* certainly did not forecast the abolition of the monarchy or the destruction of the nobility; in that sense, the historians who contend that the French Revolution was a political accident driven mainly by contingent causes have a point. But big and important reforms clearly were anticipated, and one does not have to look hard for signs of social friction and the sorts of resentments to which Sieyès gave voice. The content of the *cahiers* converge on many of the same issues, and express much agreement between the orders. Common agenda items for both the nobility and the Third Estate included the establishment of regular meetings of the Estates-General, the protection of civil liberties, freedom of the press, the elimination of monopolies, and no new taxation without popular consent. Nobles and commoners also largely agreed on the need to equalize the tax burden and to end or mitigate many forms of legal privilege.

The nature of noble privileges, however, proved to be a source of serious disagreement. Tellingly, the noble *cahiers* remained virtually silent on the "feudal" regime that gave landlords financial advantages and a range of jurisdictional rights over the peasants living on their estates. Aware of the unpopularity of that regime, noble electors seem to have agreed to avoid explicit mention of the subject; by contrast, Third Estate *cahiers* drawn up at the parish level, informed by peasant discontent, railed against the system and against the tax collectors and middle men who enforced it. Many noble *cahiers*, as already noted, expressed a willingness to give up longstanding tax exemptions. But as for honorific rights, nobles insisted that they should retain all of them. They guarded jealously their ranks and titles, membership in chivalric orders, precedence in official ceremonies, the right to wear a sword in public, deferential forms of address —in short, all of the everyday symbols of noble preeminence in the social order.

Yet the brute fact of noble preeminence in the existing order underlay the whole political fight over the composition and procedures of the Estates-General that had been raging since the fall of 1788, an early indication that even casual affirmation of the nobility's superior standing was likely to engender conflict. Sure enough, the *cahiers* drafted by the Third Estate in 1789 provide evidence that the nobility's privileged access to distinguished positions —in the army, in the church, in municipal offices, in the royal bureaucracy— had burrowed into the Third Estate's consciousness as a generative grievance, the master source of all that was wrong in the social and political order. Frustrations over the closing down of channels of upward social mobility, though arguably more a matter of perception than of reality, fed the sharpest divergences between the *cahiers* of the Second and Third Estates. Disagreements over the nobility's favored treatment in French society, and over their privileges of birth, proved to be even more contentious than the basic question of representation in the Estates-General. Sieyès's January complaints about the "vast aristocracy which overruns every part of France", bestowing "every form of contempt" on the commoners who aspired to parity in the life of the nation, anticipated the tenor of many Third Estate *cahiers*. By moving the discussion about the relationship between nobility and nation beyond the narrow parameters of the debate over representation, *What is the Third Estate?* had tapped into a deep reservoir of resentment. That resentment would soon reach a tipping point.

"So inevitable yet so completely unforeseen"

On May 5, 1789 the deputies to the Estates-General convened at Versailles in the ornate *Salle des Menus Plaisirs* (a building for decorative objects, sporting equipment, and art supplies used in court entertainments). There they heard welcoming remarks by Louis XVI and Necker. Such an air of expectancy encircled this event, and the deputies from all three orders approached their duties with such determined optimism, that thoughts of violent conflict remained unimaginable to all concerned. The sequence of events that would unfold in the following months was indeed "unforeseen" at the outset of the assembly's work.

Yet the profundity of Tocqueville's characterization of the French Revolution as both unforeseen *and inevitable* has not been fully appreciated. The long-term evolution of French society since the seventeenth century, which formed Tocqueville's main focus, had made the essentially medieval inheritance of estates, privileges and divine right absolutism increasingly vulnerable to critique by the 1780s. Just as important, the eight months that preceded the convening of the Estates-General had sharpened inter-estate animosities to a degree rarely before seen. The frayed threads of the French social fabric were plainly visible to the men charged with representing a society that had gone unrepresented since 1614.

2. Palace of Versailles, France.

As already noted, since September 1788 the pretensions of the privileged orders had inspired the Third Estate and its advocates to advance more aggressive claims to rightful political influence. The new pretensions of the Third Estate, in turn, had provoked a conservative backlash within the Second Estate. In December of 1788 the princes of the blood warned Louis XVI that "a revolution is being prepared in the principles of government", and they urged him not to acquiesce in the "humiliation of this brave, ancient, and respected nobility" that had always provided kings their firmest support. In January and February, the nobles of Brittany revolted against the efforts of commoners in that province to ensure double representation at their provincial Estates-General, and they incited bloody clashes in the streets of

Rennes. Nobles who had championed the cause of the Third Estate in 1788 began to back away from their most inclusive rhetoric well before May 1789. Exemplary in this regard was Louis-Alexandre de Launay, comte d'Antraigues, who had written a celebrated *Memoir on the Estates-General* in 1788 in which he declared that "the Third Estate is the people and...[it] is in the people that all national power resides". By the spring of 1789, he had become an adamant opponent of the vote by head; when asked to stand for election to represent the Third Estate of Paris, he refused.

The opening confrontation that defined the brief life of the Estates-General, the confrontation that would dictate the rhythm of events through the middle of July, was therefore perfectly inevitable. After the opening convocation ceremony, crown officials invited the deputies to verify their credentials —that is, to have each deputy seek formal recognition as an elected representative of his constituents. The deputies of the Third Estate refused to participate in the process. They reasonably assumed that the act of giving formal expression to their existence as an order would preclude future deliberation in common and voting by head in the assembly as a whole. They held out for a verification procedure that would apply to the entirety of the Estates-General. On May 7 they invited the clergy and the nobility to participate in a joint procedure.

The deputies of the clergy and the nobility quickly refused the invitation, and so from the very beginning of the Estates-General the privileged Estates and the commoners were placed on a collision course very much foreseeable in the months before the meeting. The failure of Louis XVI and Necker to decide the issue of voting procedures in the winter months, and the heated rhetoric that flew freely into a publishing environment newly rid of censorship in late 1788 and early 1789, created ample space for the polarization of attitudes that became evident as soon as the deputies commenced their business. Indeed, tensions became manifest even before the official convocation. At a religious service held on May 4, when the deputies first set eyes on one another, conspicuous differences in dress drew wide attention. The king's master of ceremonies had prescribed a dress code for each of the three orders. Deputies from the First Estate wore their professional attire, including capes, cloaks, and cassocks. Nobles wore plumed hats with lace cravats and golden brocade on their vests. The deputies of the Third Estate had to settle for unembellished black suits and hats. This vivid visual expression of social estate prompted one journalist to describe the "distinction of orders" as the "original sin of our nation". Consciousness of legal difference reached new heights among the delegation of commoners.

The impasse between the privileged orders and the Third Estate could be broken only by way of bold, even revolutionary, action. After weeks of futile negotiations, no doubt prolonged by the indecisiveness of a king whose intervention everyone awaited in vain, the Third Estate gravitated to the position first articulated in January by the *abbé* Sieyès, which he now forcefully repeated in his capacity as an elected representative of the Third Estate of Paris. On June 10 the Third Estate sent a final invitation to the first two orders to join them in a single assembly. One week later, having persuaded only a few parish priests to defect from the First Estate and join their company, the Third Estate deputies and their new allies declared themselves a National Assembly. This dramatic act of June 17, the climactic resolution of the tensions present since the inception of the Estates-General, asserted the sovereignty of the nation. It also set in motion the equally dramatic and sometimes violent repercussions of July and August with which the French Revolution is most closely associated in popular memory.

Crisis and Royal Capitulation

The creation of the National Assembly resolved one constitutional issue, at least provisionally, but it also created a new one. By following through on Sieyès's script and making themselves the representatives of a self-sufficient and authoritative nation, the deputies of the Third Estate had at least nominally sent the nobles and the clergy to the margins of political life, from which they could extricate themselves only by making common cause with the former Third Estate. But the National Assembly also presented itself as a rival to, or even as a replacement of, the monarch, who still regarded himself as sovereign. The king, who had been an oddly absent figure in the political ferment that swept over the country between August 1788 and June 1789, now resurfaced as an independent actor of great importance. His actions from mid-June to mid-July showed that the stand-off between the commoners and the privileged orders had not been definitively resolved after all. Louis XVI now began to act as an arbiter, though one with a clear bias in favor of an aristocracy he had formerly resented as an obstructive force.

The king's entry into the debate over who had the right to represent what —he locked the deputies of the "National Assembly" out of their regular meeting hall on June 20 and announced that he would deliver a clarifying speech on June 23— coincided with the appearance of a fourth independent actor in this brewing revolution: the "people". There was overlap between the people and the *public*, that abstract and anonymous entity whose authority had been invoked by countless writers and political figures for many years, not least of them the minister Necker. But unlike the public, which was imagined as a vector for informed opinion or the vessel that crystallized the popular will, the people were flesh and blood generators of action. In the provinces, during the summer of 1788, the people had provided a portent of the role they would come to play when large crowds protested Brienne's May edicts and even attacked royal soldiers. And in Paris in April of 1789, high bread prices and rumors of wage cuts had led to destructive riots in the Faubourg Saint Antoine, an industrial district that was home to a large working class population.

In June, however, the people began to assert themselves in novel ways, namely, as interested political actors free to express their own passions and will. By virtue of their proximity to the epicenter of political debate in the summer of 1789, the people of Paris, and for a time the people of nearby Versailles, were particularly well-positioned to announce the new popular dimension to the developing French Revolution. By early June the deputies to the National Assembly, still calling themselves the delegation of the Third Estate, had opened their deliberations to the public. When deputies used "disrespectful language" against the government or the deputies from the other orders, raucous visitors cheered them on, goading on the delegates "to say things little short of treason", according to one British observer of June assembly deliberations.

The "People" Activated

Feeling newly empowered by the convocation of the Estates-General-turned-National Assembly, and seeing the stakes of the debates held there, everyday citizens kept informed of events turned out to observe and influence the course of those events, and emboldened the National Assembly in the process. The king's sudden intervention in political debates in the second half of June, a development that promised either an affirmation of the Third Estate's claims to represent the nation or a repudiation of them, ensured that popular agitation would only increase in the weeks to come. Each day throngs of people crowded into the Palais Royal, a thriving commercial hub that had become the city's central gathering place, to hear the latest news and consume the pamphlets and broadsheets churned out by the printshops. The new atmosphere of permissiveness even induced peasants to brazenly poach game from the royal hunting grounds near the palace of Versailles in the last days of June. Louis XVI now had to contend not only with presumptuous representatives but also with a populace inclined to support them through word and deed.

The king did not have to wait long to see how determined the deputies of the former Third Estate had become since the final breakdown of their negotiations with the privileged orders. His decision to lock out the deputies on Saturday June 20 provoked them to stage one of the most vivid and memorable events of the first phase of the Revolution. Repairing to a nearby tennis court, the only available meeting site large enough to accommodate such a large gathering, they collectively took an oath not to end their work until they had provided the nation a written constitution. This demonstration of solidarity as a National Assembly —Jacques-Louis David's commemorative portrait of the event placed the *abbé* Sieyès calmly seated at the center of the canvas— found new expression at the meeting of June 23, where the king gave his much-anticipated address. He assured the deputies that he was committed to fiscal equality and to the principle of popular consent to taxation, but he rejected what he saw as the revision of France's traditional constitution and the assembly's illegal seizure of his own authority. After condemning the deputies' appropriation of the term National Assembly, and after insisting that the deputies of the three Estates should separate and reconvene in the morning, "each in the chamber set apart for your order", Louis XVI had his master of ceremonies give the order to adjourn the day's meeting. Members of the former privileged orders complied with the request, but the self-styled National Assembly refused to budge. The comte de Mirabeau, a noble representative of the Third Estate of Provence who was poised to embark on a brilliant career as a Revolutionary orator, informed the king's officer that "the assembled Nation can take no orders". The deputies would be dispersed, he added, only "by the force of bayonets".

Whether the famously indecisive Louis XVI lost his nerve that day or resolved to embrace a longer-term strategy for undermining the objectives of the Assembly, he passed up the opportunity to violently suppress the rebellion he now clearly had on his hands. The political winds shifted immediately. The majority of the former First Estate joined in the deliberations of the National Assembly on June 25, and the next day they were accompanied by forty-seven nobles. On June 27, in a humiliating reversal, Louis XVI ordered the holdouts from the First and Second Estates to merge with the larger assembly. The dramatic confrontation with Mirabeau and his colleagues on June 23 had provided the king a chance, his last good chance, to nip the Revolution in the bud. Instead, four days later, he signaled his capitulation to the demands of the National Assembly. Or so it briefly seemed.

The People's Rescue of the National Assembly

Louis XVI spent the next two weeks creating anxiety through his enigmatic silence and his ominous repositioning of royal troops. On June 26, the day before he ordered "his loyal clergy and his loyal nobility" to join the National Assembly, the king called in reinforcements in anticipation of popular unrest. Parisians became aware of troop movements to the north by the first days of July, and rumors about the king's intentions began to spread through the streets. Other troops were positioned outside Versailles, where the deputies of the National Assembly also began to wonder about the king's true designs. By July 13 roughly 30,000 new troops had been stationed in and around Paris. When the Assembly asked the king to explain his perceived need for military support, he wrote the presiding officer a terse but worrisome message. "You can assure the Assembly of the Estates-General [note the refusal to utter the words National Assembly] that the [troops] are intended only to put down, or rather to prevent, new disorders". If "the Estates-General" took umbrage at the troop presence, he added, he would happily move the Assembly to Soissons (about sixty miles northeast of Paris), while also relocating the royal court to his chateau at Compiègne. The king's statement, with its subtle tones of disrespect and hints at provincial exile for the deputies, "aroused murmurs" in the assembly hall.

Proof that the king had only been buying time since his pivotal address on June 23 came on the afternoon of July 11, when the king sacked all of his reform-minded ministers, including Jacques Necker, who was ordered to leave the country at once. News of this event, which would reach Paris the next day, caused a sensation. In the National Assembly, the deputy Mounier saw conspirators at work. Evil advisors to the king, who were interested only in "keeping the French people in servitude", had turned him against "virtuous ministers worthy of public veneration". These evil advisors would have included Marie-Antoinette, the queen's favorite the duchesse de Polignac, and the king's brother, the comte d'Artois, who were suspected of lobbying behind the scenes for more severe measures against those who had dared to challenge royal authority. In a state of alarm, the deputies at Versailles and the people of Paris all assumed that Necker's dismissal portended a military crackdown. As a precaution, many deputies chose not to sleep in their own homes on the night of July 12. They expected to be arrested or worse. The deputy Henri Grégoire anticipated that the National Assembly would soon be "inscribed in the annals of martyrdom".

The days of anxiety and uncertainty that stretched from the end of June to July 12 are still remembered two hundred thirty years later mainly because of the extraordinary way in which the uncertainty was finally brought to a close: with the Parisians' storming of the Bastille prison on July 14, forcing the king's second capitulation to the will of the people's representatives. These days helped to define the character of the French Revolution for another reason that requires emphasis, however. The trust deficit that hobbled much of the work of the Revolution over the long term can be traced directly to Louis XVI's secret surrender to the conservative forces who opposed reform between June 23 and July 11. Louis XVI would repeatedly benefit from the sort of face-saving excuses conjured by Mounier, who claimed that "virtuous ministers" like Necker had fallen because those who wished to "protect abuses" had "surrounded the throne" and contaminated the king's thoughts. But whether he succumbed to pressure or followed his own instincts, Louis XVI clearly acted in bad faith in the days after June 27, when he had recognized the legitimacy of the National Assembly by ordering the recalcitrant noble and clerical deputies to join it. The king dissembled and quietly plotted against the Assembly for the next two weeks, establishing a pattern —publicly saying one thing and secretly doing the opposite— he would follow repeatedly over the next three years. The king's failure to act in good faith gave encouragement to the forces of reaction and planted seeds of fear and doubt in the minds of all who supported the Revolution. Between July 12 and July 14 the king's stealth maneuvering caused genuine panic. More than any other individual, he was responsible for the divisive political dynamics that carried the Revolution in the direction of paranoia and authoritarianism by 1793.

In the short term, however, the feelings of mistrust would be subsumed by the widespread euphoria that accompanied the popular victory at the Bastille. On hearing word of the dismissal of their hero Necker, who had become a symbol of the people's cause, crowds gathered in the Palais Royal to listen to the latest rumors and to plot the city's defense against the expected military invasion. The journalist Camille Desmoulins evoked the Saint Bartholomew's Day massacre of 1572, fruit of an earlier treacherous plot hatched at the royal court, and he exhorted the crowd to prepare for the imminent onslaught of the king's troops. Recognizing that emergency measures would be required to meet the military threat, and hoping to prevent chaos, the 'electors' of the city —those who had elected the Parisian delegation to the Estates-General back in May— stayed in permanent session and began coordinating the city's preparations.

Because bread prices had been surging since the weak harvest of 1788, it is unsurprising that the crowds' first actions were directed against the recently constructed customs barriers that ringed the city's walls. These toll booths, manned by agents of hated tax farmers, stood as emblems of dearth and high prices. After destroying one of the dozens of customs gates they razed or burned, the crowd's search for provisions led them to the nearby monastery of Saint-Lazare, with its cellars reputed to be filled with grain. They ransacked Saint-Lazare on the morning of July 13, carrying away fifty-three cartloads of grain, and then moved on to the Hôtel des Invalides, a hospital for military veterans whose commandant capitulated without a fight. At the Invalides the crowd seized thirty-two thousand muskets, and it was the search for the gunpowder needed to fire those muskets that led them finally to the Bastille.

The Bastille prison, whose black legend had made it a symbol of despotism since early in the eighteenth century, served no important strategic purpose either for the monarchy or for the Parisian crowd that seized it. On July 14 it held only seven prisoners and only a hundred or so soldiers were on hand to defend it. The drama that unfolded there, however, provided instant and enduring symbols of a righteous political cause and of the pivotal transfer of authority from king to nation. About one thousand Parisians, most of them artisans and shop-keepers, though also including women, children, sympathetic soldiers, and a handful of merchants, participated in the assault on the Bastille. The governor of the fortress, the marquis de Launay, earned infamy when he appeared to order his troops to fire on a crowd that had surged into the inner courtyard of the prison, killing scores of innocents in the process. The crowd laid siege to the prison for hours in the afternoon of July 14, but when a contingent of French guards (a regiment nominally in service to the royal household) arrived in support of the people Launay promptly surrendered. Parisians rushed into the fortress to free the prisoners and seize the powder stored there, and over the next several hours and days they gave ritualized expression to the people's victory over tyranny. That royal troops had either refrained from intervening and halting the crowd actions of July 13-14 or had actively participated in them was itself an important sign of the people's newfound political authority. But the euphoric crowd set out to enact in self-conscious ways its new political power.

Parisians spontaneously organized a triumphal march to the Hôtel de Ville (City Hall), taking with them, like a conquering army, all the spoils of their victory, including flags, guns, armor, liberated prisoners, and the captive marquis de Launay. Sometime before reaching the steps of City Hall, the crowd executed Launay and severed his head from his battered body —thus performing rituals of capital punishment and bodily disfigurement associated with the king's legal authority. They also seized and executed a key municipal official who had been suspected of impeding the search for armaments on July 13. Placing these two heads on pikes, they then paraded them through the streets of Paris, displaying the symbols of their fearsome power.

Other reversals would follow over the course of the next several days. When, on the morning of the 15th, Louis XVI learned of the taking of the Bastille, he went to the National Assembly to announce his decision to pull the troops back from Paris. Next, after discussing with his closest councilors the impracticality of mounting a counter-attack against the city, given the suspect loyalties of the troops, he announced on July 16 the dismissal of his new ministers and the recall of Necker. This was the clearest signal of the king's unconditional surrender. The National Assembly had emerged from the crisis with its hand strengthened, its will supreme. Finally, Louis XVI informed the newly formed city government of Paris that he would visit the city in person on July 17.

For centuries, elegant royal entry ceremonies in important French cities had served both as rituals of submission to royal rule and as displays of mutual affection between crown and subjects. In a departure from business as usual, however, the new mayor of Paris, Jean-Sylvain Bailly, met the king and his small delegation outside the gates of the city. He spelled out for Louis XVI, in some of the most memorable lines uttered in 1789, the import of what had occurred in the capital since July 14. "Sire, I bring to your majesty the keys of your good city of Paris; these were the same ones presented to Henry IV [in 1594, at the end of the Wars of Religion]. He had reconquered his people; here it is the people who have reconquered their king". The Austrian ambassador, witness to the event, noted that on the long march to City Hall there were "few cries of 'Long live the king,'…whereas on all sides there were shouts of 'Long live the nation'".

Louis XVI would acknowledge the victory of the conquering people by processing to City Hall, waving to the assembled crowd from an upper story balcony, and pinning to his hat a red, white, and blue rosette. This new symbol of the Revolution, which would proliferate after the middle of July, signified the reconciliation of Paris, with its red and blue coat of arms, with the monarchy, whose traditional color was white. Draped in such unifying symbolism, and benefiting from the relative calm with which this momentous shift in power and authority had been effected, by all appearances the relationship between the king and his people had healed instantly. Optimism overcame the intense feelings of betrayal that had fueled the march on the Bastille. The National Assembly would soon anoint Louis XVI the "Restorer of French Liberty", and its deputies would begin the constructive legislative work of the Revolution.

Beneath the surface, however, trouble lurked.

Chapter 3
Division and Mistrust in a World Remade

In towns and burgs all across eastern France, large and boisterous crowds lined the streets to catch a glimpse of the carriage of Jacques Necker as he returned from Switzerland in late July 1789. In Paris a jubilant crowd gathered on the sprawling plaza in front of City Hall and hailed him as a hero. At every step on his journey, wrote one Genevan official, Necker's presence brought the "renewal of the most touching scenes, all the way to Versailles". The chief minister would soon learn that having the status of living symbol carried risks as well as advantages.

There were other signs of popular enthusiasm in the wake of the fall of the Bastille. Curious onlookers turned out in droves to witness the dismantling of the fortress, and to hear the (mostly fictional) stories about the human remains found in the bowels of the prison. Thousands of volunteers joined the urban militia —now rechristened the National Guard— that had been convened by the Parisian electors and put to work on the evening of July 13. The force was placed under the leadership of the marquis de Lafayette, veteran of the American War for Independence. Since members of the National Guard had to supply their own uniforms, only men of some means could join, but the battalions in Paris and across the country had little trouble filling their ranks in the first weeks after the mid-July crisis. An engaged readership also fueled an explosion in newspaper production in the weeks after July 14, as journalists rushed to sate the appetites of citizens eager to follow the work of the strengthened National Assembly. The Palais Royal continued to bustle with activity, and political clubs such as the "Society of Friends of the Constitution" (later called the Jacobins, after the Dominican monastery where they first met) began to organize regular meetings.

Optimism was in the air, but deep fissures in the body politic remained. Although public discourse about the king sounded notes of affection and gratitude, the fraught circumstances in which the people of Paris had fended off a likely military invasion left scars that would become easily inflamed. High bread prices continued to afflict Paris and other cities, and doubts about the reliability of the king and the aristocrats who surrounded him at court stirred unrest in the countryside. Fears of an aristocratic backlash after July 14 converged with hunger and anxieties over the grain supply to spark a "Great Fear" (so named by the historian Georges Lefebvre) that spread from village to village. There were uprisings in the east and the northwest within days of the fall of the Bastille, and by the first days of August virtually the entire country had been affected. Rumors about bands of "brigands" burning crops and destroying granaries generated spontaneous collective action that radiated throughout the provinces. In some cases, rioting peasants sought reassurances and promises of help from their noble landlords. In other cases, they destroyed legal titles, chateaus, and other visible symbols of aristocratic power over the land. Several landlords were killed. No one was left untouched by the surge of panic.

The Night of August 4 and its Aftermath

As deputies of the National Assembly received word about the disorders in the countryside, some reflected on the sentiments expressed in the *cahiers de doléances*, particularly the strong peasant resentments toward the feudal regime that still governed use of the land throughout much of the country. Anxious to curb the lawlessness that had overtaken the rural hinterlands, and also ready for an opportunity to bolster the National Assembly's authority, some of the more liberal-minded noble deputies planned a dramatic session for August 4. In response to a motion to issue a decree in favor of the "sacred rights of property", the vicomte de Noailles and the duc d'Aiguillon stepped to the rostrum and announced the repudiation of their seigneurial dues (customary payments that peasant tenants had to render to their landlord in addition to the rent set by their lease). This seemingly spontaneous show of magnanimity sparked an unanticipated parade of renunciations over the next several hours. Privileges of all kinds were thrown onto the figurative bonfire, and before the night was over the entire scaffolding of privilege undergirding the social order had gone up in smoke. Anxious about the rural unrest, delirious with patriotic fervor, and feeling newly committed to the project of national renewal, the deputies of the National Assembly had destroyed an entire regime —the prior, or former, regime (*Ancien Régime*) as it now came to be called.

Once the powerful sense of euphoria had passed, it took several days for the Assembly's deputies to sort through and codify all of the destructive work they had carried out on the night of August 4. On August 11 the deputies at last issued a formal decree announcing that the Assembly "entirely destroys the feudal regime". This decree enumerated all of the privileges —those of corporations, provinces, and municipalities in addition to those possessed by individuals— that would henceforth cease to exist, many of which would be "redeemed" at prices to be set by the Assembly at a future date. The decree of August 11 also, in effect, established much of the agenda of the National Assembly in the coming months, since the dismantling and replacement of the existing regime of privilege formed the essence of the constitution-making that remained the Assembly's reason for being.

Significantly, the August 11 decree was preceded by another decree, released on the 10th, that focused on the need to restore order. The creative work achieved on the night of August 4 had unfolded in an atmosphere of real and threatened popular violence, and in this sense the "Great Fear" enveloped the deputies at Versailles as much as the peasants in their villages. The Assembly had been debating the general issue of popular violence since the aftermath of Launay's murder on July 14. Reports of lynchings by heedless mobs on the outskirts of Paris had prompted an investigation by Assembly delegates on July 20. Then, on July 23, two former government officials, Bertier de Sauvigny (thought to be responsible for bread shortages) and Joseph Foullon de Doué (the person initially slated to replace Necker on July 12) met a horrible fate on the steps of Paris's City Hall. Like Launay, they were killed and partially dismembered before being paraded around the city in imitation of the celebratory executions that followed the fall of the Bastille. News of these vengeful murders reached the National Assembly at about the same time as the first reports of rural riots and chateau burnings. Most deputies in the Assembly had excused and even endorsed the popular violence of July 14 as having been necessary to secure the people's liberty. The prospect of the wholesale collapse of law and order nevertheless left them shaken.

The rhetorical thrust of the August 10 decree is revealing. Aware that the rural uprisings had been spurred by unfounded rumors about roving bands of brigands laying waste to the food supply, the Assembly pointed the finger at unidentified conspirators who had wished to foment "disorder and anarchy". They called on all local militias and public officials to be vigilant, to keep lists of known "disreputable persons", and to take all measures necessary to preserve the public peace. In what may be seen as a symptom of the political landscape's disorienting volatility, and of the deputies' search for new political moorings at a moment of structural disruption, the Assembly also required that members of militia units swear two separate oaths. They would first swear, "between the hands of their commandant", to serve faithfully the cause of public peace and the defense of the citizenry. The second vow would be an "oath to the nation and to the king, the head of the nation". Soldiers would swear "before their entire regiment" to be faithful to the nation, the king, and the law, and not to order actions against fellow citizens except at the express request of civil authorities.

In its appeal for calm and its recourse to oath-taking, the decree of August 10 provides a powerful reminder of the always two-sided nature of revolutionary activity in 1789. The fruitful work the National Assembly carried out in the Revolution's first summer took place in an unsettled environment where many lived in perpetual fear for their safety. The threatened violence of the royal troops in early July had been neutralized, but the counter-violence mustered by the people, which had been central to the victory over tyranny, raised fears about popular license. With traditional ties of obedience losing meaning and established authorities under constant challenge, how would the sometimes-violent impulses of the people be held in check?

Claiming Rights

The anxieties revolving around this fundamental question would churn beneath the surface of legislative debate before bursting into the open in the next pivotal confrontation of the Revolution's first year. Before that confrontation, however, the National Assembly would manage its other signal achievement of the summer of 1789: the passage, on August 26, of its *Declaration of the Rights of Man and of the Citizen*. Draft declarations, written by dozens of individuals, had been circulating through the Assembly since early July.

> The destruction of the feudal regime on August 4 had increased the urgency to craft a general statement of principles, since the Assembly had now to embark on the project of building a new regime from scratch. The *Declaration* that emerged from the Assembly's negotiations was short and remained generally on the level of the abstract. Its radicalism, however, cannot be overstated. The insistence, for example, that "every public agent" owed society "an account of his adwministration" flew directly in the face of centuries of secretive traditions surrounding the operations of government; it gave institutional sanction to the principle of transparency. The assertion that all men are "free and equal in rights" delivered a seismic shock the practical and philosophical implications of which continued to roil the social order for years to come. The *Declaration* also foregrounded the essential sovereignty of the "nation" and emphasized that the law must conform to the "general will" of the people, thus acknowledging the collective rights of the community as a whole. The *Declaration of Rights* inspired passionate loyalty to the cause of the Revolution among many; it frightened and offended many more. The abbé Augustin Barruel characterized the very idea of locating sovereignty in the nation as "insane".

The *Declaration* sought to secure the fundamental liberties of speech, expression, and religious observance, but its language repeatedly placed ambivalent checks on those liberties. All were entitled to the free expression of their opinions, for example, so long as "their public demonstration does not disturb the public order established by law". Every citizen likewise had the freedom to "speak, write, and print". But each citizen was also "answerable for abuses of this liberty in cases determined by law". The *Declaration* thus implicitly preserved for the legislative power the ability to curtail the rights of those considered to be threats to the public good.

Even in the text of the emancipatory *Declaration of Rights*, then, one finds evidence of a fault line running through the developing political culture of the Revolution. Disagreements about the appropriateness of popular intervention in the political debates of the day, and over the scope of license to be granted individual citizens in the exercise of their political rights, would bubble to the surface repeatedly in the months of September and October, and indeed throughout the course of the Revolution. The taciturn king, still suffering a kind of political paralysis after his ignominious retreat from the forces of Revolution in mid-July, temporized throughout August and September. Both his brother, the comte d'Artois, and the queen's confidante, the duchesse de Polignac, had emigrated in late July, and the isolated king once again played for time. While the National Assembly debated such matters as the content of its *Declaration of Rights*, the question of whether future assemblies should have two chambers or one, and whether the king should have veto power, Louis XVI simply ignored the National Assembly's ratification of its repudiation of privilege and the feudal system on August 11. He also refused to endorse the *Declaration of the Rights of Man*. At the end of the month, after nervous and noisy agitation in the Palais Royal, the regiment of French guards sought a confrontation with the king's bodyguards, who were rumored to be working secretly against the popular cause; only the intervention of Lafayette and a National Guard unit prevented their march on Versailles.

As the debate over the royal veto reached its crescendo, in mid-September, a new journalistic voice announced its arrival in Paris. Jean-Paul Marat, a physician and newly minted democrat who had begun to worry about the strength of counter-revolutionary forces in France, began publication of his *Parisian Publicist* (soon to be renamed *Friend of the People*), a newspaper that would later distinguish itself for its bloodthirsty defense of the people's rights. In September and early October 1789 Marat aimed much of his vitriol at Necker, accusing him of cajoling the king to stand firm in defense of his full executive powers. The man who posed as a champion of the people, according to Marat, was in fact a "Satrap of a despot", one always ready to bargain with the enemies of the Revolution. Marat and other journalists also criticized Mounier and deputies allied with him, the so-called *monarchiens*, who wanted to preserve the king's power over law-making and advocated an absolute royal veto over legislation from the Assembly.

The deputies struck a key compromise on September 15 by granting the king a suspensive veto, meaning he would need to sustain his veto through three separate legislatures elected in successive rounds of voting. Louis XVI then exacerbated tensions by signaling immediately that he would not support the decree of August 11 without modifications. He conveyed this message to the Assembly through Necker, who therefore took some of the blame for the king's stubbornness. A further ratcheting of tensions occurred a few days later when Louis XVI, rattled by the earlier aborted threat from the French guards, called to Versailles reinforcements from his Flanders regiment, known for its fierce loyalty to the crown. Soon after the regiment's arrival rumors swirled in Paris that some of the Flanders officers, celebrating at a welcoming banquet held in their honor, had insulted the "nation", declared that their fealty was to the king alone, and trampled underfoot a tricolor rosette. The story was probably exaggerated, but it ignited fear and outrage in the streets of Paris and helped to provoke a popular action that would prove to be a turning point.

The October Days

The scarcity of bread, in the weeks before the harvest of 1789, had raised tensions throughout September. Apprehensive because of the king's failure to support either the *Declaration of the Rights of Man* or the decree of August 11, and newly fearful of a possible "counter-revolution" (the word first appeared around this time) that could undo the work of the National Assembly, the women of Paris organized a march on Versailles for October 5. Eventually joined by the marquis de Lafayette and several battalions of the National Guard, who were anxious to maintain order while also preserving their legitimacy in the eyes of the crowd, about ten thousand women marched to the royal palace and forced themselves into the courtyard. There they beseeched the king to supply Paris with bread. In the wee hours of October 6, a number of women and National Guardsmen breached the interior of the palace and even threatened the safety of Marie-Antoinette, who feared for her life. Lafayette calmed the passions of the crowd and persuaded Louis XVI to address the throng from a balcony overlooking the courtyard. There the king promised to fortify Paris's grain supply, and he seemed buoyed by the spontaneous shouting of "Long live the king!" that greeted him, but the Parisians would not be satisfied unless king and queen agreed to return with them to Paris. Sensing that a refusal could lead to bloodshed and the endangerment of his family, Louis XVI agreed to leave Versailles for the Tuileries palace adjacent to the Louvre, in the center of the city. He and the queen made the long journey, now accompanied by tens of thousands of giddy celebrants, during the afternoon of October 6. The deputies of the National

Assembly followed the royal party to Paris in the weeks that followed, taking up quarters in a dormant riding academy on the palace grounds.

These "October Days" —the first of the post-Bastille crowd actions that would come to be referred to simply as momentous "days" (*journées*)— drove a wedge in the Revolution that would never be removed. Experienced as an exhilarating victory by the people who led the march, the events of October represented a humiliating defeat for the king and for those who had been trying to shore up royal authority since the shock at the Bastille. Louis XVI had been forced to assent to both the *Declaration of the Rights of Man* and the August 11 decree, an affront to his authority from which he never recovered psychologically. During the chaotic moments on the morning of October 6, two of his personal guards had been killed, their heads severed and paraded on pikes on the grounds of the royal palace. On the road back to Paris, he and Marie-Antoinette endured insulting chatter from disrespectful activists who, with bread on their minds, celebrated their victory over "the baker and the baker's wife". He would later recall that his forcible relocation to the Tuileries represented not only the loss of his authority but also the loss of his liberty.

Nor was it only the royal family that looked aghast at the behavior of the crowd in October. Jean-Joseph Mounier, who had authored the Tennis Court Oath in June and had been presiding over the National Assembly on the day the women marchers arrived from Paris, abandoned the Revolution in the wake of the October Days. Unable to countenance the scenes of disorder at Versailles —made worse in his mind by their association with women acting out of place— he retired to Dauphiné before emigrating to Switzerland in 1790. Most of his *monarchien* colleagues likewise declined to join the other deputies at the Tuileries, thus inaugurating a process of political splintering that inexorably undermined the unity of the National Assembly and its successor bodies. (Loose political parties began to form in the fall of 1789, with ardent Revolutionaries sitting on the left-most side of the gallery and their opponents seated on the right —the origin of the modern division between "left" and "right" wings in global politics). The patriotic effervescence that had surged unexpectedly through the Assembly on the night of August 4, bonding the deputies through dedication to a common cause that transcended all earlier political differences, would never be recaptured.

The October Days also sparked a second wave of aristocratic emigration, this one large enough to give critical mass to *émigré* communities across the borders of the Austrian Netherlands to the northeast and of Savoy to the south. From those bases, anti-Revolutionary activists began to lay plans to restore Louis XVI to his full powers. In late December an accomplice of the comte de Provence, the king's conservative brother, was arrested on suspicion of arranging loans to fund an invading counter-revolutionary army, one seeking to liberate the king and queen from their captivity at the Tuileries. When the alleged intriguer in this shadowy conspiracy, the marquis de Favras, went to the gallows in February 1790, his death was cheered by thousands of supporters of the Revolution who rejoiced to see a nobleman executed not on the chopping block but by hanging —an ignominious punishment formerly reserved for commoners.

The violence and uneasy resolution to the October Days thus brought to the fore several overlapping crises of legitimacy, crises that would vex the Revolutionary project for years to come. For the king and for all who sought to retain for the monarchy some vestige of the authority kings had wielded before June 1789, the crowd's assertion of the right to control even his movement and whereabouts, not to mention his forced acceptance of the Assembly's August legislation, rendered Louis XVI a king in name only. The legitimacy of the monarch's constitutional authority, already in flux given the unfinished state of the constitution, lay at the mercy of an unpredictable crowd. At the same time, all of the aristocratic *émigrés*, and many other conservative-minded people both inside and outside the National Assembly, and inside and outside of France, rejected the legitimacy of the crowd's implicit claim to have a power superior to that of both king and Assembly. The Anglo-Irish statesman and man of letters Edmund Burke, provoked to write his caustic and influential *Reflections on the Revolution in France* (1790) by the shock of the October Days, shuddered at the thought of a king and queen forced by "ruffians" to abandon a sanctuary "left swimming in blood, polluted by massacre". For opponents of the Revolution, memories of the October Days, and the specter of crowd action that the event represented, provided all the sustenance their resentments would ever need. Finally, as the Assembly worked through late 1789 and 1790 to remake France's administrative organization, its municipal politics, its relationship to the Catholic church, and most of its laws, its legitimacy, too, was buffeted by unrelenting pressures from political clubs, newspapers of both the right and the left, and a restless populace with high expectations.

Progress and Peril

Mutual suspicion, and fears of counter-revolution and possible civil war, cast a pall over all the work of 1790 and early 1791, despite the Assembly's steady progress in implementing the principles articulated in the summer of 1789. The old provinces of France, possessors of privileges and mobilizers of regional identities, were abolished and replaced by eighty-three rationally designed administrative "departments", roughly equal in size and population. In a move that would have pleased Turgot or Calonne in earlier times, the deputies sought to spur economic growth by eliminating the tolls and customs duties once enforced by provinces and municipalities. Suffrage rights were expanded, though not nearly as far as champions of popular activism would have liked. The Assembly's distinction between "active" and "passive" citizens —only the former, able to pay annual taxes equivalent to three days' wages for an ordinary laborer, were accorded the right to vote— would prove divisive until the August Revolution of 1792. Still, in winter and spring of 1790 municipal elections around the country introduced many citizens, over half of the adult male population, to local electoral processes that helped to increase their investment in the work of the Revolution.

Easily the most divisive measures taken by the National Assembly involved the Catholic church. Already in November 1789 the Assembly had announced its intent to expropriate from the church all of its considerable landholdings. The precipitating cause of this move was the need to address the still pressing problem of the state debt. The Assembly issued paper money (a move Necker opposed), called *assignats*, whose total collective value approximated the total value of landed property owned by the former First Estate (about ten percent of the country's land). The state would exchange these interest-earning bonds for specie or various forms of outstanding state debt, and individuals who acquired the *assignats* could use them to buy church lands as they gradually came on the market. This stratagem provided an ostensibly solid backing for the leftover debts of the *Ancien Régime*, and those who purchased newly available church property also gained new reasons to support the Revolution. Within six months of their original issuing, however, by late 1790, the *assignats* would begin to lose their value. Inflationary pressures would cause new headaches for successive Revolutionary governments.

The Assembly had expropriated the lands of the church for another reason essential to the principles of the Revolution, at least as the majority of the deputies understood them. The church's role as default moral agent in the polity —distributor of charity, trainer of young minds, manager of hospitals, object of moral veneration— was to be displaced, in part, by the regenerated French state. Hence the landed wealth the church had long used to sustain its various educational and charitable activities should now rightly pass, so went the thinking, to the organs of the state. This logic dictated much of the National Assembly's policy toward the church throughout 1789 and 1790. Tithes had already been abolished in the decree of August 11, and full civil and political rights were extended to Protestants in December. In February 1790 the Assembly abolished monastic vows, since supreme loyalty (the Assembly would later make clear) should be directed toward the nation rather than to any religious institution.

In July 1790 the Assembly promulgated the Civil Constitution of the Clergy, a highly controversial measure that made explicit the state's superiority over the church. Clergy were now to be considered civil servants of the government, and elective principles would be introduced into the ecclesiastical hierarchy. Parish priests were to be elected by their parishioners; bishops were to be elected by priests. All would collect a salary from the state, in recognition of the valuable civic duties they performed. In November 1790 the Assembly went one step further. In an echo of the decree of August 10, 1789, which had required members of local militias to take an oath of loyalty to the nation, the Assembly imposed on clergy, in a decree of November 27, 1790 the obligation to swear "to be faithful to the nation, the king and the law, and to uphold with all their power" the constitution agreed upon by the Assembly and the king.

The imposition of the clerical oath was one of the great unforced errors committed by the National Assembly. It gratuitously aggravated religious tensions in a country where the vast majority of the population still thought of themselves as good Catholics. The expropriation of church lands had certainly been controversial, but the promise of salaries for clergy and the state's vow to replace the critical services formerly provided by the church had kept most Catholics at least nominally on the side of Revolutionary reforms. The imposition of a loyalty oath brought slowly simmering tensions to a boil. Asking clergy to commit unconditionally to a constitution not yet written, one that would inevitably complicate clerics' allegiance to the Roman see, proved a bridge too far for roughly half of the clergy in France. "Refractory" priests, as those who rejected the oath would be called, became symbols of the divisiveness of the Revolution; they would also become active sources of counter-revolution.

Until the second half of 1790, the counter-revolution, despite the generally hapless efforts of the comte de Provence and his allies, existed more in the imagination than in reality. But the imaginations of the Revolution's supporters had been given ample fuel by developments in the first half of the year. The trial and execution of Favras in February proved that fears of aristocratic plotting had a basis in reality. In early April, the National Assembly's Committee on Pensions began to release details of its investigation into a secret Red Book (*Livre Rouge*), a court register of royal pensions and gifts doled out to the favorites of Louis XVI and Marie-Antoinette since the 1770s. Readers were scandalized to learn that finance ministers had long ago created a secret category of disbursements "in order to hide an infinity of expenses that [the state] would have been ashamed to admit to", as the chairman of the committee put it.

Secret betrayals had been essential ingredients in the royal court's misuse of state funds, as the people had been told at least implicitly as far back as Necker's *Account to the King* in 1781. (Necker's apparent complicity in the accounting that lay behind the Red Book, which seemed to make him guilty not only of secrecy but also of hypocrisy, contributed to his swift decline in popularity over the course of 1790). In the eyes of Revolutionaries, secrecy had grown only more sinister since the machinations of the king and his conservative advisors in early July 1789 had prompted the assault on the Bastille. So it seemed a propitious coincidence when, just one week after the Committee on Pensions disclosed its first revelations from the Red Book, Parisians learned of a secret meeting called by conservative members of the National Assembly. The *abbé* Jean-Siffrein Maury and André vicomte de Mirabeau, the younger brother of the famed orator, convened a large evening gathering of like-minded conservatives at the Capucin church on the rue St.-Honoré in Paris. At this nocturnal "sabbath", as Desmoulins described it, they discussed a legislative strategy to have the Catholic church declared the official state religion, thereby preventing the appropriation of church lands. They also schemed to discredit "patriots" in the Assembly.

3. Statue of Queen Marie-Antoinette in the basilica of Saint-Denis.

By early the next morning, a vigilant journalist had published a brochure —*Assembly of the Aristocrats at the Capucins: A New Plot Unveiled*— and outraged Parisians, on reading its panicked rhetoric, showed up to hector Maury on his walk to the National Assembly's meeting hall. They filled the gallery to listen to Assembly deliberations and to ensure that the motion to declare Catholicism the state religion would be defeated. To the author of *Assembly of the Aristocrats*, the meeting at the Capucins represented much more than the natural byproduct of legislative debate. "Citizens, do you not see the triumphant air of the aristocrats, do you not hear their insults? Have you not witnessed their insolent joy? Do you know the cause? It is because they think that the counter-revolution, toward which they have worked with such ardor, has now ripened. They think it is time to harvest the fruits [they have cultivated]". Huge sums of money had been removed from the Royal Treasury in recent days, the author reported, and the "horses in the king's stables have been readied". Desmoulins repeated this rumor, and raised the specter of the king's imminent flight, in his influential *Revolutions of France and of Brabant*.

The fear of counter-revolution and aristocratic conspiracy helps to explain the other dramatic piece of legislation passed in the summer of 1790, just weeks before the Civil Constitution. On June 19, two days after the Assembly heard its first formal report from the Committee on Pensions concerning the abuses detailed in the Red Book, the deputies of the National Assembly unexpectedly moved to abolish all titles and marks of hereditary distinction. The fate of noble titles had not been on the announced agenda for this Saturday evening session, and many noble deputies had not bothered to come. The debate was therefore heated but short, with the marquis de Ferrières observing that "one could neither hear nor be heard" over the tumult. With a handful of liberal nobles leading the charge, within minutes the institution of nobility passed out of existence. This measure, too, seemed gratuitous to many. Ferrières noted that the night of August 4 and the elimination of social estates in the fall of 1789 "had already effectively destroyed the nobility". In light of this reality, the marquis asserted, "there remained no distinctions other than those rooted in opinion". The Assembly's repudiation of even the honorific use of personal titles, and the denial of any vestige of social superiority in French social life, alienated many former (*çi-devant*) nobles who, to this point, had tried to make peace with the Revolution.

Desiring both to move toward political closure and to neutralize growing fears about concealed enemies, the National Assembly, by its own dramatic actions in the summer and fall of 1790, made the counter-revolution an enduring reality. More than myth or psychological projection, in late 1790 and early 1791 the counter-revolution became a semi-cohesive movement with the clear goal of undoing the great changes that had occurred since July 1789. The Assembly had put meat on the skeletal specter of counter-revolution by creating two distinct populations of Revolutionary victims —the refractory priests and the nobility, both of whom would count disproportionately among the roughly 150,000 emigrants who fled France in the decade of the 1790s. The expulsion from the Revolutionary creed of both refractory priests, prioritizing their religious loyalties, and nobles, many of whom remained attached to the distinctions from which they had always benefited, meant inevitably that large numbers of both groups would drift (or race) toward the pole of counter-revolution. Signs that the center was failing to hold were already accumulating in the first months of 1791.

Polarization and the King's Flight

In the summer of 1789 Jacques Necker had stood as a beacon of hope for all pro-Revolutionary constituencies, a stabilizing presence who represented the ascendancy of public opinion, if not exactly of the popular will. By the summer of 1790 Necker's support in the National Assembly had evaporated, and his reputation was under assault for reasons having more to do with the new atmosphere of suspicion than for anything he had actually done. Bruised by the controversy over the Red Book, forced in late 1789 and early 1790 to issue successive reports indicating revenue shortfalls and the need for new loans, and increasingly mistrusted simply by virtue of his position next to a suspect king, Necker found himself without influence even over financial matters by summer 1790. When the Assembly decided, against his recommendation, to issue more than a billion *livres* in *assignats*, and to declare the bills legal tender across the entire country, the Genevan submitted his resignation and quietly returned to his Swiss estate at Coppet. One of the potentially unifying figures of the early Revolution had departed the scene demoralized and defeated, a victim of circumstance, his moderate political instincts, and unprecedented political volatility.

The other figure who had often tried to steer a middle course through the first years of the Revolution, Necker's rival the comte de Mirabeau, was also largely a spent force by the early months of 1791. An often-inspiring orator, Mirabeau had emerged as an early leader of the National Assembly in summer 1789. As a nobleman clearly committed to constitutional monarchy, but one also courageous enough to defend the cause of the National Assembly against royal threats in June and July 1789, he had the ability to mediate between different factions in the Assembly and even to negotiate with the king and his agents. Hungry for influence, however, he overplayed his hand by angling for a position as royal minister in the weeks after the October Days. He had already tried to play both sides in the debate over the royal veto; by positioning himself as a possible savior for constitutional monarchy after the October crisis, he made himself suspect to his fellow deputies in the Assembly. The Assembly decreed in November 1789 that the status of minister was "incompatible" with that of deputy. As the deputy Adrien Duquesnoy observed in his recollections about the key vote on incompatibility, "No matter what art is used to cover it up, ambition always breaks through; [Mirabeau's] maneuvers do not escape observant men".

Whatever his standing in the Assembly, however, in July and August of 1790 Mirabeau engaged in regular meetings with Louis XVI, Marie-Antoinette, and the Austrian ambassador Florimond Mercy-Argenteau, a confidant of the queen's. Alarmed by the radical turn in the Revolution, Mirabeau was still hoping to craft a *modus vivendi* that would save the constitutional monarchy while retaining some of the liberal principles outlined in the *Declaration of the Rights of Man*. That compromise solution never materialized, but it is clear that all four principals in these discussions of summer 1790 had begun to envisage the prospect of civil war. Mirabeau and Mercy-Argenteau had also begun to think about extricating the king and the queen from Paris. When the National Assembly passed its decree requiring clergy to swear an oath to the constitution in November, Louis XVI signaled to key advisors his own support for the idea of breaking away from the capital. Necker, Camus, Mirabeau, Desmoulins, Louis XVI, Marie-Antoinette, Mercy-Argenteau and many lesser figures understood that they confronted a dangerously, perhaps inescapably, polarized political environment in France by the middle of 1790.

When Mirabeau died prematurely on April 2, 1791, at the age of forty-two, the event was one of several to act as a catalyst for the king and queen as they contemplated the terms of their departure from Paris. A number of unsettling encounters with Parisian crowds in this same period also reminded the ever-temporizing Louis XVI of the volatility of the people, underscoring for him the unacceptable conditions that had been imposed on the royal family since the October Days. In one particularly harrowing encounter, on April 18, Parisians gathered at the gates of the Tuileries to prevent the royal family from decamping to their nearby chateau of Saint-Cloud for their planned celebration of Easter services. The crowd was determined to prevent the king from attending Easter mass with refractory priests. In the course of the confrontation, several of the king's retainers were treated roughly by the crowd, the National Guard troops failed to disperse the crowd even after Lafayette gave the orders to do so, and insults and threats were hurled at the king himself. After a tense standoff, the king and his family turned around and reentered the palace, feeling less free than ever.

In the two months that followed the incident of April 18, the king, the queen, and a coterie of close confidants —including the mastermind of the escape plan, the Swedish diplomat and soldier Axel von Fersen, who had been on intimate terms with the queen for some years— focused their energies on planning the royal escape from the Tuileries. Several escape strategies and destinations were considered, but in the end the team decided that the king, the queen, their two children, and an unwieldy retinue of seven would sneak out of the Tuileries palace in the dead of night and head toward the northeastern fortress of Montmédy, just two miles from the Austrian Netherlands. Louis XVI would later claim that he had had no intention of joining up with Austrian forces, or of using his proximity to Austrian territory to plead for foreign assistance against the Revolution, but the decision to flee to a military fortress on the border with Austria, rather than to Normandy (the location preferred by the late Mirabeau) or to some other town or chateau in the country's interior, looked incriminating.

Royal Obliviousness

In any case, the royal family never made it to Montmédy. The failed royal flight of June 21, 1791, the details of which are authoritatively relayed in Timothy Tackett's *When the King Took Flight*, crystallizes much that defined the French Revolution during its so-called "liberal" phase of 1789-1791.

The indecisive and dilatory manner of Louis XVI proved crucial in delaying the planned escape and in ensuring that the royal party missed its rendezvous with the military escort waiting in the fields outside of Somme-Vesle, near the mid-way point of the journey. An aristocratic addiction to luxury, which had been a flashpoint of popular resentment in the years leading up to the Revolution, helps to explain the excess number of servants and the sumptuous accoutrements that slowed the travelers' progress and left them exposed on the road for longer than necessary. Royal obliviousness to the perceptions and experiences of others, best captured by Marie-Antoinette's apocryphal declaration on learning of the reality of peasant hunger ("Let them eat cake!"), accounts at least in part for the decision to travel in a large and ostentatiously yellow *berline* carriage rather than a streamlined and inconspicuous coach that would have attracted less attention. This insular outlook on the world also explains why Louis XVI so recklessly exposed himself to the view of townspeople whenever the *berline* changed horses at its designated relay stations. Blithely assuming that all who lived outside the vicious confines of Paris felt undiminished affection for him, he allowed himself to be recognized by puzzled onlookers more than once. It was one such encounter, at the town of Sainte-Menehould, that ultimately led to the king's capture, near midnight, at the border town of Varennes.

At Varennes, the king's party had to confront another of the essential realities that defined the "liberal" phase of the French Revolution. Over the course of the previous two years, ordinary people had become so politicized, and they felt such pride in nation, that an ill-prepared and misguidedly confident king and queen could prove no match against them. On the morning of June 22, the garish *berline*, with its precious cargo, was launched under heavy military escort back in the direction of Paris.

Popular Activism, Rights, and the Constitution

When Parisians heard the news of the king's flight, and of his capture at Varennes, a wave of nervous anticipation swept over the city. In the minds of many, Louis XVI's decision to abscond from the capital only confirmed a history of bad faith maneuvering on his part. At two moments in the course of 1790, first during a speech to the National Assembly in February and then again at a great festival celebrating the one-year anniversary of the fall of the Bastille, the king had sworn his allegiance to the nation and the National Assembly. He had promised to honor and uphold the constitution still in the making. Many, and perhaps most, of the people of Paris and across the country provisionally chose to suppress their doubts and to opt for hope in the wake of those public declarations. But few could shake the memories of Louis's previous untrustworthiness —from the unexplained closure of the National Assembly's meeting hall in June 1789 to the secretly planned military invasion of Paris in July to his obstinate refusal, in the prelude to the October Days, to accept the National Assembly's legislation of August. To many, the king's attempted flight signaled a simple return to form. The journalist Elisée Loustalot, primary editor of the popular newspaper *Revolutions of Paris*, showed little surprise in reporting that "this cowardly, treacherous conspiracy, hatched for the last eighteen months, has at last been carried out".

And indeed, in a note Louis XVI had left behind on his desk on the evening of June 21, written in his own hand, he made clear his sentiments about the Revolution. Noting that he had "solemnly protested", to no avail, all actions taken by the National Assembly during his "captivity", he implored "Frenchmen, and above all Parisians", to "return to your king". Once reunited, king and people could work toward a different constitution that, he wrote, "will cause our holy religion to be respected,...the property and status of each one no longer to be troubled, [and] the laws no longer to be disobeyed with impunity". In other words, the king would undo the Civil Constitution of the clergy and the abolition of nobility. He would also ensure that episodes of popular violence and other instances of illegality, no matter the political stakes involved, would be summarily punished. When word of the king's letter reached the Parisian populace —copies were printed in every newspaper and the streets buzzed for days— many expressed revulsion at the king's dishonesty.

The king's flight could not have happened at a more sensitive time for the National Assembly. The deputies were only weeks away from finalizing the constitution that had been in the works since August 1789, and plans for new legislative elections were already under way. Worse, the constitution they had nearly completed placed the monarchy at its center. All of the deputies had been assuming since the fall of 1789 that Louis XVI would become the first constitutional monarch in French history. The king's abandonment of the capital, and his repudiation of most of what the Revolution had so far accomplished, set off a politically and emotionally frenzied four-week period during which the fate of the king, the constitution, and the Revolution itself all seemed to be at risk. The fallout of the captured king's return to Paris constituted a crisis —one of a series of related crises that would rock France's government to its foundations between 1791 and 1793.

The questions that demanded the immediate attention of political leaders after the king's return on June 25 ostensibly focused on the nature of the executive power in the new regime. Should Louis XVI remain on the throne? Should he be replaced by his son? Should France remain a monarchy? The uncomfortable resolution the National Assembly improvised in response to these basic questions would leave a cloud over the government that would last for many months. But the event of the king's flight and return was momentous not only because of its implications for the mechanics of governance. This event changed the French Revolution because it also happened to intersect with an ongoing development fueled by energy generated outside the halls of the legislature. For months before and after the king's flight a wide-ranging debate carried out largely but not exclusively in the streets of Paris focused on the true meaning of the *Declaration of the Rights of Man and of the Citizen*. A craving for new and more widely shared rights percolated through the streets for much of 1791.

The ground-level political activism that had begun to lay down roots in 1789 had mushroomed in the years since. Political clubs and fraternal societies had proliferated since the fall of 1789, with as many as one thousand clubs in existence across the breadth of the country by the end of 1791. One of the hallmarks of the Society for the Friends of the Rights of Man (or Cordeliers Club), the most influential of the Parisian political clubs that emerged in 1790, was the promotion of an egalitarian politics not particularly well reflected in the composition or work of the National Assembly. Unlike the more exclusive Jacobin Club, for example, the Cordeliers Club, led by radicals such as Desmoulins, Marat, and Georges Danton, charged only nominal membership fees and actively recruited "passive" citizens, including women, as participants. Indeed, one of the priorities of the Club in the spring of 1791 was to pursue the abolition of the distinction between active and passive citizens and thus to make male suffrage rights virtually universal. They were supported in this program by members of the forty-eight Parisian "sections" that had been created in the spring of 1790 to handle electoral processes in the capital. The local sections, hosting a representative cross-section of the Parisian populace, quickly mutated into all-purpose organs of political activism, and since they operated virtually without interruption they became organizational vehicles for radicalization whenever new threats to the Revolution emerged. The sections, the Cordeliers Club and the fraternal societies they sponsored, as well as other political clubs in Paris, actively sought to influence the work of the National Assembly in its waning months. They hoped to push the Assembly toward a more expansive definition of citizenship and a more capacious understanding of rights. This backdrop of ongoing political agitation provided a crucial ingredient of the context in which the fate of the king and the constitution would be decided in June and July of 1791.

Another sign of the continuing fermentation of the principles of 1789 was the decision of the National Assembly, in May 1791, finally to wade into colonial politics after having determinedly ignored the practical and philosophical problem of slavery in French territories since the summer of 1789. The Assembly reaffirmed its promise to the white planters of Saint-Domingue (the future Haiti), Martinique, and Guadeloupe that it would refrain from meddling in the legal status of enslaved persons unless invited to do so by the Colonial Assemblies dominated by the slaveholders themselves. Nevertheless, by a decree of May 15, 1791 the Assembly extended to free people of color whose parents had also been free —a minority within the minority— the right to sit in parish and colony-wide assemblies. Buckling to renewed pressure from the agents of white planter interests who remained in Paris, the Assembly would rescind the decree of May 15 in September. By then, however, a slave rebellion had erupted at Saint-Domingue, changing the political calculus in profound ways, as will be noted in chapter four. The attention devoted to the issue of citizenship rights in the colonies in spring 1791 had already shown, however, that the *Declaration of the Rights of Man and of the Citizen* clearly remained a work in progress.

One of the few ardent promoters of outright abolitionism in the first years of the French Revolution, the playwright Olympe de Gouges, further amplified the debate about rights when she published, just weeks after the National Assembly completed its constitution in September of 1791, her *Declaration of the Rights of Woman and of the Citizen*. Modeled after the *Declaration of Rights* adopted in August 1789, it too had seventeen articles —one of which attacked the "perpetual male tyranny" to which women had been subjected. Each article appropriated for women one of the rights ostensibly secured for men in the text of the original *Declaration*. ("Woman is born free and lives equal to man in her rights", read Article One). The *Declaration* was then followed by a philosophical postscript that took aim at the ideological foundations of marriage ("the tomb of trust and love"), inheritance law, the mandate of priestly celibacy, and other patriarchal institutions. Gouges closed her brochure with a nod to the free people of color in Saint-Domingue. Liberty, she declared, must "hold the National Assembly to its decree [of May 15], dictated by prudence and justice". Only stout advocacy for the former slaves could bestow the full blessings of liberty on Saint-Domingue, for "there is where reason and humanity have still not touched callous souls".

The ideological ferment and robust popular activism of 1791 help to explain why the flight of the king, and the National Assembly's confused handling of his forced return, proved so pivotal to the French Revolution. Both the popular reaction to the king's return to Paris, and the authorities' management of the popular commotion, underlined the degree to which popular sentiment had evolved beyond the thinking of the majority of the Assembly. In the last week of June, the Cordeliers Club and their many supporters flooded public gathering sites in Paris and marched to the National Assembly's meeting hall on several occasions. There they demanded that the Assembly either suspend the king and declare a republic or place the question of the king's fate on a referendum ballot so that all French citizens could weigh in on the future of the monarchy. It quickly became clear to the marching activists, however, that the deputies in the National Assembly had little appetite for reconsidering the wisdom of their two years of hard work on the constitution. Although a handful of deputies, including Maximilien Robespierre, were sympathetic to the demands of the crowd and would remain permanently mistrustful of the king, even they saw the writing on the wall and were disinclined to disrupt the process of completing and ratifying the constitution. Each new petition submitted by the political clubs was met with an attitude of haughty dismissal in the Assembly's chambers. Frustrations finally boiled over in mid-July.

The Cordeliers Club, on July 12, took the unprecedented step of seeking to bypass the authority of the National Assembly. They announced that they would send an "Address to the Nation" calling for immediate legislative elections and for the constitution of a new executive authority, comprised of one delegate from each of the country's eighty-three departments, to replace the king until his ultimate fate could be determined by referendum. Voting in all cases would take place in accordance with universal male suffrage rights.

4. Motto "Liberté, Egalité, Fraternité", town hall of Paris, France.

This attempt to circumvent the authority of the National Assembly, which would prove moot in just a few days' time, reflected not only continuing frustrations over the deputies' failure to act on popular petitions. Worse, the Assembly seemed prepared by the second week of July to fabricate excuses for the king that would allow him to pose as a misunderstood supporter of the constitution the Assembly had crafted. Specifically, deputies cynically accepted the false story, offered up by an exiled general who had been involved in planning the king's flight, that Louis XVI had been abducted, persuaded against his will to leave behind on a temporary basis his good people of Paris. This failure of nerve enraged many, but a majority of deputies ultimately decided, on July 15, that this determined embrace of false consciousness was the price to pay to preserve the stability of the government and to forestall further popular agitation.

By early July, the anger of populist agitators toward the National Assembly had come to be fully reciprocated, as the deputies in the Assembly began to fear the destabilizing potential of further popular unrest. The mutual animosities led to a decisive clash on the fabled Champ de Mars (an outdoor gathering site near today's Eiffel Tower) on July 17. The Cordeliers Club had organized a final surge of pressure they wished to direct at the National Assembly. Throughout the day on July 16 they had spread the word that there would be a huge gathering on the Champ de Mars the following day, a Sunday, to sign one more petition —this one calling on the Assembly to revisit their ill-considered decision to exonerate the king and to arrange for his replacement by a new form of executive. Deputies in the Assembly, alarmed at the presumptuousness of the crowds, urged the mayor of the city, Bailly, to take matters in hand and to mobilize troops against the unruly Parisians should the people fail to come to their senses. Feeling pressured, Bailly declared martial law and marched off to the Champ de Mars with Lafayette and multiple National Guard units at his side. Accounts of the event are confused and conflicting, but it appears that troops from the National Guard panicked when someone from the crowd fired a shot in the direction of Bailly. Advancing into the field, the Guard troops opened fire without warning and killed dozens of bystanders and unarmed protesters. When the smoke had finally cleared, the crowd had dispersed but the reputations of both Lafayette and Bailly —among the last of the reputed moderates who could lay claim to some credibility as Revolutionary leaders— lay in tatters. Neither would ever recover from the stain left on their hands by the blood of innocents on the Champ de Mars.

Disagreements over the appropriateness of the Champ de Mars protest and of the crackdown that followed would soon split the Jacobin Club. Moderates such as Antoine Barnave and Adrien Duport, who had been stalwarts at the Jacobins throughout the spring of 1791, left to form their own political club, the Feuillants, whose chief purpose was to defend the constitutional monarchy against its many radical challengers. Meanwhile Robespierre, Jérôme Pétion, and other populists remained in the Jacobin Club and tilted its orientation more decisively in the direction of support for the Parisian crowd and mistrust of Louis XVI, who was formally reinstalled as king in early September after accepting the final draft of the constitution devised by the National Assembly.

5. Maximilien Robespierre.

These ideological differences between Feuillants, on the one hand, and the Jacobins and Cordeliers, on the other hand, also showed up in the work of the National Assembly in its final weeks. Wary of seeing a repeat of the organized protests of late June and July, when the Assembly's chambers had been invaded by angry crowds on several occasions, the Assembly outlawed collective petitions. In one of their final acts as a legislature, the National Assembly also worked to limit the impact of the clubs in the nation's political life. As the deputy Isaac-René-Guy Le Chapelier explained it, "everyone wants the Revolution to be ended". Closure could not be achieved, however, if people persisted in intruding upon legislative decision-making. A hopeful Le Chapelier urged his fellow deputies to take satisfaction in demonstrable achievements. "The time of destruction is past; no abuses remain to be abolished, no prejudices to combat". Clubs therefore had to abandon their public character and cease their coordination. Clubs should facilitate the private meeting of minds only, not the forms of collective agitation capable of threatening a government now organized on Revolutionary principles. Robespierre doubted the wisdom of breaking "an instrument that had served us so well", but the moderates nevertheless carried the day in the Assembly. The decree limiting the activities of clubs passed, though it would never be formally implemented.

The period between August 1789 and July 1791 had seen the creation of a new constitution for France. Revolutionaries had swept away a venerable social order established since the Middle Ages, fundamentally changed the relationship between church and state, altered the political geography of France, and empowered millions of people in ways unthinkable as recently as 1787. But the National Assembly did not bequeath a stable political settlement to its successor body, the Legislative Assembly. The deputies of the National Assembly, in a hurry to finish their work, retained monarchical institutions, and they even retained the person of a monarch disgraced in the eyes of a large percentage of the population. Whether because of nerves or because of uncertainty over the broad principle of people power, they also missed the opportunity to establish a workable and trusting relationship between "the people" and their government. For these reasons, and also because of the difficult circumstances created for them by the king's betrayal, the National Assembly in the summer of 1791 inadvertently charted a path toward instability and violence. By the time the deputies in the Legislative Assembly had taken their seats at the end of September, new violence outside of France and new agitation for violence inside France were already roiling the legislative waters.

Chapter 4
War and the Republican Turn

The late summer and fall of 1791 inaugurated a new phase of the French Revolution. This new phase was defined less by the transfer of power from National Assembly to Legislative Assembly, though the differences between the two Assemblies proved to be significant, than by the intrusion into the revolutionary dynamic of events taking place beyond French borders. In the closing months of 1791, the French Revolution was fully internationalized. The dramatic consequences of this turn would change both the character and the course of the Revolution.

Reverberations across Borders and Oceans

In fall 1791, the French government found itself drawn deeply, and largely against its will, into the internal affairs of its colony in Saint-Domingue. The free population of this economically vital island colony —including rich plantation owners, free people of color, and the poor whites who resented both— had been sparring for many months over the effects of the French Revolution in the colony. Initially, only the rich planters derived any benefit from the Revolution, as they were granted token representation in France's National Assembly. But the promulgation of the *Declaration of the Rights of Man* raised the political stakes of the Revolution for all inhabitants of the colonies. The white planters in Saint-Domingue formally prohibited circulation of printed copies of the *Declaration of Rights*, and in a rearguard action designed to protect their economic privileges, their colonial assembly declared independence from France in 1790. Back in Paris, the National Assembly neutralized this threat by assuring the white planters that it had no intention of meddling in the "status of persons" on the island.

The Assembly's May 1791 decree extending rights of representation to some free people of color in the colonies came in response to intensifying claims on the part of Parisian agents of the free blacks of Saint Domingue. They had been pushing since late 1790 for a more inclusive reading of the *Declaration*'s core principle that men are born "free and equal in rights". One of these men, Vincent Ogé, frustrated by the lack of progress at the National Assembly, had returned to Saint-Domingue in late 1790, where he sparked an uprising of free blacks in the North Province of the colony. Although he made it clear that he had no intention of extending freedom and equality to the island's enslaved population —Ogé, like many other free blacks, had been a beneficiary of Saint-Domingue's slave-centered economy— Ogé's rebellion against the government in Cap-Français nevertheless caused great anxiety among the white planters. They sent a professional military force in pursuit of the rebels, and they eventually were able to bargain with Spanish forces in neighboring Santo Domingo, where Ogé had fled, to secure possession of the rebel ringleader. He met his end in the public square of Le Cap after a gruesome ordeal during which he was broken on the wheel, separated from his head, and displayed to onlookers as an example of the fate that awaited insurgents. If the white planters hoped that the public spectacle of Ogé's execution would mark an end to their troubles, however, they judged badly. News of Ogé's rebellion, and of the brutal punishment meted out to him by the colonial government, encouraged both opponents and proponents of the idea of legal equality to mobilize new efforts in support of their respective causes. The National Assembly's surprising May 1791 decree, which followed days of intense debate, grew in part out of revulsion at the manner of Ogé's execution.

The white planters nevertheless used the specter of armed revolt to put renewed pressure on the National Assembly to rescind its May decree, and they succeeded. In one of its final decisions, the National Assembly reversed course on September 24, 1791 and canceled the decree they had voted on in May. By that time, however, conditions on the ground in Saint-Domingue had rendered obsolete the legislative debates about the electoral rights of free blacks. In late August, the enslaved people of the North Province of the colony initiated an uprising of their own. Aware of the seething tensions setting white planters against the free blacks, and hearing talk of the ongoing political commotion in France, slaves were also affected by a rumor that the French king had already tried to extend them new freedoms only to have those efforts blocked by a recalcitrant colonial assembly. Restive since April, when an initial uprising dissipated before it really began, on the night of August 22, 1791, the slaves finally took advantage of the social and political fissures that had been deepening on the island since late 1790. Their best-informed leaders had been laying plans for a revolt for some time. Those plans were set in motion during the evening of August 22, when hundreds of sugar plantations were set ablaze. In turn, news of the slave uprising galvanized the free people of color, who now rose in rebellion in the West Province. As the white owners of large plantations in that region began to bargain with the free blacks, in hopes of securing their assistance in putting down the slave revolt, poor whites became all the more determined to reject such an alliance. Wishing to uphold a racial hierarchy that at least preserved their legal if not their economic superiority over free people of color, they continued to fight the rebellious bands of free blacks throughout the fall of 1791. Port-au-Prince would be left in ashes in November, and both the slave uprising in the north and the rebellion of free blacks in the west drifted toward military stalemate by the end of the year. They would remain fixed there throughout much of 1792 and 1793, as French metropolitan authorities belatedly tried to fashion a coherent response to the crisis in Saint-Domingue even as they confronted a series of new crises at home.

These other crises also flowed from the increasingly urgent need to manage the relationship between the French Revolution and the world beyond France's borders. By the time the leaders of the French Legislative Assembly heard the news about the uprising in Saint-Domingue in October of 1791, they had already been grappling with a new foreign threat that arose from the turmoil surrounding the king's attempted flight to Montmédy. For months, from his new home base in Koblenz, Louis XVI's brother the comte d'Artois had been rallying French *émigrés* and European rulers to engage in more active opposition to the

Revolution. In response to this lobbying, the Prussian king Frederick-William II and the Holy Roman Emperor Leopold II, brother to Marie-Antoinette, issued on August 27 their Declaration of Pillnitz, which threatened imminent military intervention in France's domestic political affairs. Referring to the French state of affairs as a matter of "common interest for all of Europe's sovereigns", the rulers declared their intention to render Louis XVI "totally free to consolidate the bases of a monarchical government… as amenable to the rights of sovereigns as it is to the well-being of the French nation". In pursuit of that goal, they would "issue their troops the necessary orders to prepare them for action".

In 1791 the Austrians and Prussians were in fact distracted by political developments in eastern Europe, and the Pillnitz declaration represented more bluster than reality, but the prospect of a military invasion understandably caused great trepidation in France. The looming threat posed by foreign armies and the French citizens assumed to be their allies dominated the activities of the Legislative Assembly in fall 1791 and shaped the entirety of its brief, ten-month life. The Assembly moved quickly against Artois and the *émigrés*. They first issued a decree that denied the king's brother his right of succession to the throne and then appealed to the archbishop-elector of Trier to disperse the French *émigrés* gathered at Koblenz. Another law against the *émigrés*, passed in November, threatened state confiscation of their properties if they failed to return home before the end of the year. Next the deputies took aim at refractory priests, passing a law that required them to come forward to swear their oaths to the constitution or risk exile from France.

These measures were designed to undercut the budding counter-revolution through legislative threat, but bolder alternatives soon presented themselves. Louis XVI, in his first dramatic actions as a constitutional monarch, vetoed the legislation against refractories and *émigrés*, thereby making his long-term intentions officially suspect in the eyes of many of the deputies in the new Assembly. The composition of this Assembly was much different from that of the National Assembly with whom the king had finally reached an uncomfortable *modus vivendi* in July. For one thing, there was no overlap in their membership. According to a "self-denying" ordinance passed by the National Assembly in May 1791, no members of the National Assembly could stand for election to its successor body. The ulterior motive behind the ordinance was to permanently remove from the legislative process those obstinate remnants of the First and Second Estates who had opposed the Revolution and had failed to keep step with the times. An important consequence of the law, however, was that voters placed in office a much younger and less experienced group of legislators at a parlous moment for the developing Revolution. New to the process as they were, the deputies were more easily swayed by the strong arguments advanced by the most prominent personalities among them.

Among the most prominent was Jacques-Pierre Brissot, a pamphleteer and journalist who had founded one of the most successful newspapers of the Revolution's first year, *The French Patriot*. Brissot had also spent time in both England and America, had been impressed by the statesmen of the new American republic, and had founded in 1788 the Society of the Friends of the Blacks, France's first abolitionist group. Active at the Jacobin club, and immersed in Parisian municipal politics, Brissot needed little time to get acclimated to the rough and tumble business of legislating in a high-stakes environment. Cosmopolitan, eloquent, and boasting unimpeachable revolutionary credentials, he quickly became a leader within the Legislative Assembly. In short order he gathered around him a group of allies contemporaries came to call the *Brissotins*.

What this meant in practice was that the Legislative Assembly drifted steadily toward war. Moderates certainly existed in the Assembly —the Feuillant club, formed in the aftermath of the king's flight, maintained a robust presence there— but the suspicious Brissot had reacted viscerally to the Declaration of Pillnitz and he soon began advocating for a preemptive war against the Revolution's foreign enemies. When the Austrians added fuel to the fire in December by pledging military support for the elector of Trier should he be harassed further over the presence of French *émigrés* in his territory, Brissot took to the pages of *The French Patriot* to ask a rhetorical question that guided his thinking in the months that ensued. "Will we wait, then, for all the tyrants of Europe to be ready to attack us, before thinking of attacking them ourselves? Frenchmen! Forward!"

The Pressures of War

Preparations for war would constitute forward progress, in Brissot's mind, for at least three reasons. First, the military effort would harness the revolutionary energies of the people and provide a unifying objective that could overcome lingering domestic tensions. Second, through war the French could export the liberating force of their Revolution, leading a "crusade of universal liberty" —a thought no doubt encouraged in the mind of this precocious abolitionist by the recent developments in Saint-Domingue. Third, and most urgently, the prospect of a life or death struggle with the forces of counter-revolution would smoke out from their dens all who were secretly conspiring against the cause of Revolution at home, beginning with the king himself. "I have only one fear", Brissot thundered at the Jacobin club, namely, "that we shall not be betrayed. We need great treasons". The exposure of great treasons would prompt salutary remedies, since there remained "great doses of poison within the heart of France and violent explosions are needed to expel them".

Brissot guessed correctly that the agitation for war would stir the passions of citizens eager to defend the *patrie*. The established symbols of the Revolution, such as the tricolor rosette and the red cap of liberty, became ubiquitous over the course of spring 1792 (and the guillotine would make its first appearance in April). Brissot had been only half right, however, about Louis XVI. The king and queen indeed continued their secret machinations with the Holy Roman Emperor, the elector of Trier, and the comte d'Artois. But the king cagily refused to show his hand. He played along with the Legislative Assembly's warmongering, installing a team of ministers in March 1792 who were all close to Brissot. Bowing to the legislative will, he even preemptively declared war on the emperor on April 20 —though he did so precisely because he expected the Austrians and their allies to lay waste to the under-prepared French army and to march to the rescue of royal authority in France.

The tension between Louis XVI's publicly professed support for the war and his private but widely suspected desire to see the war end badly for France increased steadily throughout the spring and summer of 1792. The war started inauspiciously for the French, as the army suffered several losses in rapid succession across the border in the Austrian Netherlands. Hearing news of mutiny and unrest on the border, and approaching something of a state of panic, the Legislative Assembly passed two laws in late May and early June that aimed to facilitate the self-defense of the capital city. The first would have made it easier to order the exile of refractory priests; the second called for the formation of an encampment of National Guardsmen, called in from all over the country, to be stationed along the perimeter of Paris where they would be prepared to repel the Austrians or their Prussian allies should they advance on the capital. The king, typically, temporized. Baffled by the lack of royal urgency, Louis's interior minister, Jean-Marie Roland, warned him that unless he acted immediately, "a grieving people" would come to look upon their king as "the friend and accomplice of conspirators". Unmoved, Louis responded to Roland's effrontery by dismissing Roland and the rest of the Brissot-friendly ministry (June 13) and by vetoing the new laws (June 18).

Two days after his veto, a crowd of Parisian artisans, laborers, and shopkeepers —they had come to be called *sans-culottes*, laboring people who did not sport the fancy knee-breeches of the upper classes— forced their way into the Tuileries palace and confronted the king over his refusal to defend the capital. In its essentials, this confrontation represented a replay of the summer of 1791, with an angry Parisian crowd rejecting the intolerable presence of an executive suspected of treachery. "The people" now asserted its moral authority against both the king and a representative assembly that had failed to take charge. And this time, events would subsequently show, the people won the contest. Even as they chanted the customary phrase, "Long live the king", they forced Louis XVI to don a Phrygian cap and to spend several hours chatting on familiar terms with the sort of people whose power had long terrified him. When the mayor of Paris arrived on the scene and persuaded the crowd to desist, they left the king unmolested and without having secured his promise to reverse his vetoes. But their defiant expression of the popular will signaled a new direction for the Revolution.

The *journée* of June 20 marked the definitive passing of the Revolutionary initiative to the common people and their advocates. Although many members of the Legislative Assembly recoiled at the sight of an undisciplined crowd harassing a king, the deputies retreated into passivity after June 20. They managed to overrule the king's veto of an encampment of National Guardsmen for the capital, but even this legislative achievement served mainly to empower a popular movement that now took on a life of its own. Armed patriots from all over the country —they were popularly called *fédérés*— streamed into the city throughout the month of July 1792, providing new activist energy for an urban population already on tenterhooks because of the imminent threat of foreign invasion. The power of both the king and the Assembly steadily dissipated as political clubs, the forty-eight sections, and National

Guardsmen from every province —lustily singing the refrains of the recently composed *Marseillaise*— issued increasingly radical demands and began mobilizing collective action against the Revolution's foreign and domestic enemies. The domestic enemies now included the marquis de Lafayette, whose determined anti-populism led him to make a clumsy attempt at the end of June to execute the ban on political clubs. His efforts went for naught, and his influence entered a period of precipitous decline even among the troops he commanded on the border. He would soon make the decision to flee the country and abandon the Revolution.

> **Constitutional Monarchy Imperiled**
>
> Both Lafayette and the majority of the Legislative Assembly could see that the monarchy, and the constitution of 1791, were now in jeopardy. The radical political clubs, as well as many Paris sections, supported by the rapidly politicized *fédérés*, began to call for the king's abdication or removal by the middle of July. In a petition to the Legislative Assembly, one section announced its readiness to "bury itself under the ruins of liberty rather than subscribe to the despotism of kings".
>
> The sense of urgency arose not only from the preparations for military invasion but also from an impatient desire to finally punish the king for his false expressions of patriotism.

> As citizens of the Mauconseil section put it in an address to the Legislative Assembly on August 4, the "despicable tyrant" had "played too long" with the destinies of the French. "Without distracting ourselves further in calculating [Louis XVI's] errors, crimes, and betrayals, let us strike at the fearful colossus of despotism, let it fall, let it break into pieces, and let the sound of its fall turn tyrants pale from one end of the earth to the other". Another deputation called for "the reign of truth" to begin. The image of the duplicitous king, concealing nefarious plots to the end, would hang over late 1792 and early 1793; the king's dishonesty, for which explosive new empirical evidence would come to light before Louis XVI's final judgment, would also shape the psychology that made possible the repressive measures of 1793 and 1794.

Before the serial crises of 1793 and 1794, however, the French had to enact the climactic confrontation that, by August 1792, no one could have failed to see coming: the overthrow of the monarchy. In another sign of the repetitious character of the conflicts of summer 1792, foreign adversaries issued yet another threatening and inflammatory decree at the end of July. Using language stronger even than that in the Declaration of Pillnitz, the rulers of Austria and Prussia pledged, in their "Brunswick Manifesto" (named for the Prussian Duke who commanded the Allied Armies and conveyed the message) "to put an end to the anarchy in the interior of France, to check the attacks upon the throne and the altar,...to restore to the king the security and the liberty of which he is now deprived and to place him in a position to exercise once more the legitimate authority which belongs to him". They warned the city of Paris that if "the least violence" were visited upon the king and queen, the invading armies would inflict "an ever memorable vengeance" that would entail "the complete destruction" of the capital. The Brunswick Manifesto, in short, promised the restoration of the *Ancien Régime* and dire punishment to all who resisted that restoration.

It would be difficult to imagine a warning more calculated to ensure Parisians' preemptive strike at the Revolution's internal enemies. The Legislative Assembly, alas, was unable to rouse itself to action; Brissot and his allies had belatedly discovered the virtues of conservatism, especially as it regarded constitutional law. In early August they even resisted calls for the impeachment of Lafayette, which only confirmed in the minds of restive Parisians that decisive action would require further popular initiative. An ad hoc coordinating committee consisting of section leaders and members of the clubs brushed aside the Assembly's refusal to act and began planning their own assault on the Tuileries. The Parisian municipal government, now calling itself the Commune, filled the void left by a Legislative Assembly fallen into desuetude and openly called for insurrection. Finally the coordinating committee, planning with officials of the Commune, agreed to move on the Tuileries on the morning of August 10.

At the ringing of the tocsin, National Guard units moved on the palace. They joined up with other Guardsmen who were stationed there, and who quickly defected from the king's side in order to join the patriot cause. Together this amalgam of *fédérés* and Parisian Guardsmen did battle with the king's Swiss Guards, who valiantly sought to protect the king's interests in the face of superior numbers and in the wake of their abandonment by the king himself, who had fled with his family to seek the protection of the Legislative Assembly next door. At the end of the hours-long *mêlée*, roughly six hundred Swiss Guards lay dead in the courtyard of the palace, the Tuileries having been vanquished and the monarchy's authority decisively repudiated by the self-proclaimed agents of the people. Back at the Legislative Assembly, Pierre-Victurnien Vergniaud, deputy of the Gironde department in southwestern France, rendered official what everyone now recognized. He declared the monarchy suspended, announced that the king would remain under house arrest indefinitely, and called for new elections —to proceed on the basis of universal manhood suffrage— to form a National Convention that would be entrusted with determining the path forward.

6. The Louvre Palace, adjacent to the Tuileries gardens, site of the definitive fall of the monarchy.

The Revolution's engagement with hostile outsiders, imagined as a galvanizing and potentially purifying ordeal at the beginning of the year, had thus brought about the sudden collapse of the monarchy itself, to the surprise of both Louis XVI and the Brissotins. The threat posed by advancing foreign armies, and the manifest refusal of the king and, ultimately, the Assembly to take bold precautionary measures in response to that threat, had fueled new insurrectionary energies among the people and precipitated a second Revolution. The National Convention would soon make clear that this second Revolution had been republican in character, thus inaugurating a new era in French history —an era that required a new way of reckoning time itself. A newly designed Revolutionary calendar would refer to September 22, 1792 —the day the Convention officially declared France a republic— as the first day of Year I; this calendar would remain in effect until 1806.

A Triumphant Moment (attenuated by deep mistrust)

The Revolution of August 10 represented a triumph of the Parisian popular will, as well as a cathartic release of mounting frustrations over the government's handling of its emergency powers. The aftermath of the event, however, revealed sharpening divisions among the political classes over the perennial question surrounding the legitimate extent of the people's power. On the one hand, by suspending the monarchy, calling for a National Convention, and implementing universal manhood suffrage, the Legislative Assembly legitimized the attack on the Tuileries. Going further, they immediately named as justice minister the people's hero, Georges Danton, whose base of power lay squarely in the Parisian club movement. And they effectively ceded much control over national affairs to the Paris Commune, which had been radicalized as it became more and more responsive to the popular will. (A "Provisional Government" of ministers theoretically answered to the Legislative Assembly during the six weeks of its existence, but in practice it did nothing without at least the tacit support of the Commune).

The most recent expression of the people's sovereign will thus acquired the stamp of legitimacy, just as it had in the wake of the fall of the Bastille. But on the other hand, the Brissotins harbored resentment over the people's recent usurpation of the Legislative Assembly's authority; those resentments were exacerbated by measures of retribution taken against the surviving defenders of the Tuileries and against refractory priests in the weeks after the fall of the monarchy. As rumors of the Allied armies' march on Paris swirled through the sections in the weeks after August 10, spiraling fears about the imminent arrival of the Revolution's external enemies led vigilantes to round up the Revolution's suspected internal enemies and throw them in the city's prisons. The sections established "surveillance committees" to identify and incarcerate suspects, and Danton established a special Revolutionary Tribunal to judge political crimes; this Tribunal sent its first suspected traitor to the guillotine on August 21.

Thus the stage was set for one of the bloodiest, chilling, and most divisive events in the entire history of the Revolution: the 'September Days' of 1792. On August 26 word reached Paris that the Allied army had seized the fortress of Longwy, just inside the French border, and that Verdun lay next in the army's path. The news made Paris's vulnerability a visceral reality. The process of imprisoning suspects accelerated, and firebrands such as Marat even suggested the arrest of Assembly deputies, including Brissot, whose sudden moderation since July had inspired a new set of suspicions. On August 30, Danton authorized home-to-home searches ("domiciliary visits") for the requisition of guns and ammunition and the rooting out of any remaining counter-revolutionaries, and on September 2 he delivered to the Legislative Assembly one of his most memorable speeches. He called for 60,000 volunteers to march to the front in a "sublime movement of the people". At the same time he assured his audience that with "boldness, still more boldness, forever boldness", France would be saved from its enemies.

Prison Massacres

In his call for bold action from the people, and in highlighting the dangers the Revolution now faced, Danton helped to precipitate an episode of protracted popular violence in the streets of Paris. Willing to march to the front but unwilling to leave behind counter-revolutionary enemies now rumored to be plotting a coordinated prison-break, citizens of Paris moved spontaneously on the prisons. Beginning in the afternoon of September 2 and continuing through September 6, workers, section leaders, and some rogue elements of the National Guard administered vigilante justice to prisoners scattered through every quarter of the city.

> In the course of the assault, some groups of prisoners were subjected to wholesale slaughter, but most were dispatched after having been "judged" by improvised tribunals that read aloud the charges against them, rendered convictions (and also acquittals), and turned the condemned over to crowds who mercilessly bludgeoned or stabbed them to death. In all, roughly 1,400 prisoners were massacred. Many priests and remnants of the Swiss guards who fought at the Tuileries counted among the victims, but the majority of those who perished were forgers, thieves, and other common criminals who posed no threat to the Revolution.

In its ferocity, and in its blind demonization of real and imagined political opponents, the event of the 'September Days' foreshadowed the political executions that would arrive in 1793-1794, and it set off a poisonous debate —still raging three years after the event— over the people's authority to engage in extra-legal action. Nevertheless, Paris and the nation enjoyed a partial respite from divisive drama in the two weeks after the last prison execution on September 6. Elections for the National Convention had to be completed before the first gathering of that Assembly on September 20. That first meeting happened to coincide with a pivotal military victory over the Prussians at Valmy, a victory so decisive for France's new citizen army, and so disorienting for the

Prussians, that it led to a months-long Allied retreat across the border. Consequently, the first days of Year I were heady days, infused by a new optimism about the fortunes of the French army and the prospects of a National Convention that aimed to inaugurate a new era in French and human history. The new assembly soon began work on a republican constitution.

That constitution would never be formally implemented, however, and bitter disputes between the deputies, evident from the very first days in the life of the Convention, provided a revealing symptom of the fatal disunity that would finally render their constitution unworkable. In his newspaper, Brissot had been disparaging the supposed conspirators behind the September Days ever since the close of the event, and on September 24 he, Vergniaud, and a number of their allies —a group dominated by individuals from the Gironde department and hence commonly referred to as *Girondins*— sought to regain control over the Parisian street and to reassert authority over the Paris Commune. They proposed measures to crack down on "brigands" who took the law into their own hands, and they called for a new encampment of National Guards —to be drawn from a cross-section of units around the country and to be assigned the specific task of protecting the deputies of the Convention against possible incursions from outsiders. As reward for his efforts in this work, Brissot was drummed out of the increasingly radical and populist Jacobin club and subjected to a relentless campaign of denunciation in which Robespierre, Danton, and Marat all participated. Throughout the months of October and November, Brissot and his Girondin allies, on one side, and, on the other side, Robespierre and his allies —called *Montagnards* (those from the Mountain) for their habit of occupying the highest tier of seats in Convention meetings— sniped viciously at one another. They sought to delegitimize their opponents in the eyes of the public, and they angled for advantage in the National Convention, where at least half of the 749 deputies remained unaligned with any faction and were thus often susceptible to persuasion.

The enmities had become highly personal, but at their heart lay deep and principled disagreements over the power of the Parisian people. This source of division had of course been present in the revolutionary project since 1789. Still, the events of 1791 and 1792 —the massacre on the Champ de Mars, the legislative attempt to throttle the club movement, the popular take-over of the Tuileries on June 20, the sidelining of the government on August 10, and now the prison massacres of September— had turned division into chasm. In the eyes of the Mountain and its allies in the Commune and in the Jacobin club, Brissot and the Girondins were not merely champions of law and order; they were closet counter-revolutionaries who had secretly opposed the revolution of August 10 and continued to conspire against the people. To the Girondins, who enjoyed a plurality in the Convention well into spring 1793, Robespierre and company were not merely aggressive defenders of the people's rights; they were bloodthirsty anarchists who used the force of the people to pursue selfish, short-sighted, and destructive agendas.

Echoes of these disagreements over the power of the Parisian populace could be heard in the contentious debates of December 1792 and January 1793 over the fate of the king. Just as debates over the procedures for judging the king got under way, in mid-November, the deputies of the Convention found themselves in possession of a smoking gun: a large and secret cache of letters between Louis XVI and various of his co-conspirators —including the late Mirabeau and members of the Feuillant club— that spelled out in clear terms the French king's persistent scheming against the Revolution. These letters, found in an "iron cupboard" hidden behind a panel in the Tuileries palace, only recently placed there by the king himself, overdetermined the king's guilt. There could be no question of liberating or rehabilitating the king. But what was to be done with him? This question haunted the Convention for six weeks, with the key opposing positions, articulated by Vergniaud and Robespierre, reflecting incompatible perspectives on the rights and power of the people.

7. *Monument aux Girondins* in Bordeaux, France.

For Robespierre, justice demanded the king's immediate execution. Invoking the authority of those who had marched on the Tuileries, Robespierre asserted that "the great question" had already been settled by the declaration of the republic. "Louis denounced the French people as rebels; to punish them he called upon the arms of his fellow tyrants. Victory and the people have decided that he alone was the rebel". In the wake of August 10, either the king had to stand in the eyes of the law as a condemned man or the Republic would be put in the precarious position of having to defend its legitimacy. To allow Louis XVI to stand trial would be to bring "the revolution itself" before a tribunal, a prospect both practically and morally unthinkable. Having already exercised their natural "right of insurrection", the people had dissolved the social compact under which they had endured the institution of monarchy. The monarch therefore had no further rights to assert. "The trial of a tyrant is the insurrection; his sentence is the end of his power; his punishment, whatever the liberty of the people demands". And with the "savage hordes of despotism" preparing once again to "tear at the entrails of France in the name of Louis XVI", French liberty clearly demanded the king's prompt elimination.

At the root of Robespierre's position lay his conviction that the people of Paris had engaged in a sublime act of sovereignty —a re-forging of the social contract, as Rousseau might have imagined it. Recognition of the legitimacy of that act required the branding of the king as both illegitimate and as a continuing threat to the well-being of the people. Vergniaud, with Robespierre's arguments fully in mind, made a very different appeal to the authority of the people. The most eloquent and trenchant of the Girondins, Vergniaud insisted that all important constitutional decisions taken by the Convention had to be submitted for either the formal or the tacit approval of "the sovereign" —meaning all the citizens of France. And in a life or death decision involving a former king, the citizens' consent had to be formal rather than tacit. Vergniaud rejected Robespierre's argument that a decision to refer the matter to a referendum of the people would risk popular disturbances in the departments. Such fears, Vergniaud suggested, reflected Robespierre's flawed assumption that "the people" of the country at large —who were calm, dispassionate, and patriotic— in any way resembled the "brigands who, in the month of September, sought to found their power on the debris of the monarchy." The "agitators" of Paris, empowered by the "shameful weakness" of certain officials, had usurped authority they did not possess and had repeatedly carried their passions to "the most deplorable excess". For Vergniaud, then, the gravity of the issue of the king's fate required that decision-making power be dispersed throughout the country and not left in the hands of a radical Parisian populace whose supporters in the Convention would label as traitor anyone who failed to reach "the heights of brigandage and assassination".

In the end a middle path was chosen. Rejecting Robespierre's recommendation, the Convention went through the mechanics of a trial, and in mid-January the deputies voted by an overwhelming margin to convict the king of treason. Vergniaud also met disappointment, however, because the Convention rejected by a healthy margin his proposal to refer the king's fate to the people at large. Instead, the Convention itself took a roll call vote on whether to put Louis to death. By a single vote margin, deputies opted for immediate execution. 'Louis the Last,' as his more sardonic critics would refer to him, went to the scaffold on January 21, 1793. By all accounts he performed his last political act with the dignity befitting a proud and at least semi-tragic king.

The removal of the king from the French political equation, had it occurred in a vacuum, might have effected the salvation of the Revolution. Louis XVI's Janus-faced politics —in his approach to the revolutionary ferment of May-July of 1789 and in his management of revolutionary government ever since— inspired the people's mistrust; created grounds for mutual suspicion in the nation's deliberative assemblies; gave comfort and encouragement to internal counter-revolutionary forces; and offered an invitation to foreign powers who had an interest in meddling in France's affairs. Despite having been christened the 'Restorer of French Liberties' in the summer of 1789, Louis XVI had repeatedly shown himself to be a bad faith actor whose continued presence at the center of the polity could not be accommodated by supporters of the Revolution. The removal of a chief executive who had doubled as a secret enemy of his own government should have provided a much-needed moment of clarity and a newly solid foundation on which to build the first French Republic.

By the time Louis XVI went to the guillotine, however, centrifugal forces —both in the Convention and in the nation at large— had reached too advanced a state for the fragile republic to subsist without recourse to further extra-legal maneuvering. In the Convention, philosophical and strategic disagreements had been grafted onto personality conflicts and factional suspicions in ways that proved crippling. Across the country, the trauma of the king's trial and execution, the inflationary pressures created by the sputtering paper currency, and the mounting pressures of war sowed doubts about the wisdom and propriety of the pivotal decisions emanating from Paris. Order and direction would be fully restored only after one group —the radical Jacobins and their allies— successfully seized control of the right to define the meaning of the Revolution. The narrow path forward that they forged in 1793 and 1794 salvaged the war effort, gradually quieted internal dissent, and secured French independence from the republic's many foreign enemies. Opponents of the radicals' policies, however, could claim with considerable evidence that they had saved the Revolution only by destroying it.

Chapter 5
From Popular Purge to Armed Repression: Power to "the People" and Back Again

The Girondins held the upper hand in the National Convention through most of late winter and spring 1793. Had the Convention not faced a series of confounding crises during these months, one can at least imagine that they might have succeeded in achieving a normal political solution to the factional divisions that now rent the legislature. Through their powers of persuasion, they might have won over a clear and stable majority of the deputies and offered sufficient gestures of goodwill toward their opponents to forestall the festering of fratricidal hatreds. They might have avoided the escalation of animosities that increasingly made extra-legal political tactics appealing if not unavoidable. In short, the Girondins, in the wake of the king's execution, might have managed the transition to a functional representative democracy.

Alas, this was not to be. And although the personal defects and will to power of many individual deputies certainly contributed to the Convention's failure to hew strictly to legality in the spring of 1793, circumstances not entirely of the Convention's creation proved determinative. France remained at war, and the execution of the king proved to be pivotal in the Revolution's developing relationship with the international community. With the Convention having already announced in December its intent to liberate other European peoples from their oppressors, and with Belgium already under French military occupation, the other crowned heads of Europe took notice of the events of January 21. The British quickly moved to rally other governments in opposition to the metastasizing republican menace. As Danton observed on the floor of the Convention, "you have thrown down your gauntlet to [Europe's rulers], and this gauntlet is a king's head, the signal of their coming death!" To preempt a widely anticipated British declaration of war, the Convention declared war on the British just eleven days after having executed Louis XVI. A month later, the deputies declared war on Spain. In the course of March and April, Russia, Portugal, Naples, and Sardinia all joined the coalition against republican France. Throughout

1793 and early 1794, the National Convention faced existential threats from all sides.

At Risk of Implosion

Nor did the special pressures of wartime come solely from the outside. The sweeping military successes of the fall of 1792 had given way to disorder, disintegration, and defeat in the early months of 1793. Thousands of French volunteers simply returned to their homes after triumphantly occupying the Austrian Netherlands. The Austrian and Prussian forces regained their numerical footing in the west after king and emperor (in league with the Russian czar) completed their partition of Poland. And the hero of Valmy, Charles-François Dumouriez, dramatically repudiated the Convention. When the Convention sent a delegation of four deputies to carry out an inspection of his army in late March, Dumouriez turned them straight over to the Austrians; he then defected to the coalition forces on April 5, causing consternation in Paris when the news arrived. To counter this series of disasters, the Convention adopted extraordinary measures designed to stop the bleeding and to centralize emergency decision-making. One of the undeniable effects of these measures was to alienate many French citizens, especially those who were far from Paris, disoriented by the execution of the king, fatigued from the unending political drama, and resentful of the heavy-handedness of the new government.

Perhaps the most controversial measure taken by the Convention was the decision to conscript three hundred thousand soldiers to replenish the dwindling ranks of the volunteer army of 1792. A tactic reminiscent of the monarchical old regime, this mass levy required each department to produce its share of new soldiers —by drawing lots in village after village if necessary. This latest intrusion into local life sparked an organized and eventually armed resistance, particularly in the west and southwest where the great majority of rural parishes staunchly supported their refractory clergy and where royalist sympathies remained strong. The tales of mass bloodletting by rebels, and of the retaliatory bloodletting carried out by republican agents and members of the National Guard, further polarized the country and encouraged officials in Paris to take matters more firmly in hand. In and around the department of the Vendée, all out civil war raged throughout the remainder of 1793; deputies in the Convention had good reasons to wonder how far the rebellion might spread.

Facing serious military threats from inside and outside the country, the Convention lurched in an authoritarian direction. It reestablished the Revolutionary Tribunal that had been suspended in November, thus threatening all counter-revolutionaries with the penalty of death. The work of the Tribunal was supplemented by the vigilance of surveillance committees, which the assembly now established in every city and village. The Convention also sent "representatives on mission" to help direct the work of the local surveillance committees, to supervise the conscription process, and to trouble-shoot any local issues that impeded enforcement of Convention directives. These representatives on mission operated with the full authority of the Convention and often meted out severe penalties to those implicated in, or even suspected of, counter-revolutionary activity, the definition of which expanded steadily. Back in Paris, the Convention established a Committee of Public Safety (CPS) in April. This small elected committee, charged with all responsibilities necessary for internal security and for the execution of the war effort, was led initially by Danton and a group of Montagnard allies. Its powers would grow exponentially in the months ahead.

All of these emergency measures enjoyed wide support in the Convention, with some Girondins joining deputies from the Mountain in trying to engineer political stability from the top down. Ironically, however, the vigor shown by the Convention in these months —with the Girondin plurality closely associated with the assembly's work in the eyes of the populace— prepared the ground for the Revolution's next great turning point: a confrontation between the Girondin deputies and those who gave voice to the popular will of the Parisian streets. For in addition to the crises of military conflict and civil war, the Convention faced an economic crisis between February and April as high prices, a slumping *assignat*, and food shortages roiled Paris section meetings and brought violent protests. The sections demanded that price controls be placed on bread; when the Convention refused, workers rioted and plundered shops throughout the city. Just two weeks later, on March 10, a popular uprising took aim at the Convention, as radicals such as Marat channeled the hunger and anxiety of the Parisian crowd into a targeted assault on the Girondin leaders within the Convention. Brissot, Vergniaud and their allies had been operating under a cloud of suspicion ever since the summer of 1792, and they made no effort to hide their impatience with popular demands —voiced increasingly in the tenor of class war against the rich— throughout the winter of 1793. The uprising of March 10 failed, but it succeeded in provoking newly repressive measures from the Convention, which decreed the death penalty for anyone who advocated the redistribution of land. At the end of the month, the assembly also announced the death penalty for all who would incite murder or the destruction of property.

Destructive Factionalism

A combination of passionate animosities and calculated opportunism made possible the developments that would culminate in the dramatic purge of Girondin deputies. With a counter-revolutionary insurgency underway in the Vendée, and news of the unexpected collapse of Dumouriez's army recreating the panicked atmosphere of August 1792, fears of a coordinated conspiracy against the Revolution pervaded both the halls of government and the popular consciousness. So far-reaching were these fears, so dark the mutual suspicions, that the Convention voted on April 1 —ironically, at the urging of Girondin deputies— to revoke the law providing immunity from arrest to all legislators. If counter-revolutionary activity were to be exposed even on the floor of the Convention, went the thinking, the government had to possess the wherewithal to act. By coincidence that same day, April 1, saw Dumouriez betray the Convention by surrendering its special delegation of four deputies to the Austrians. When news of this treachery, executed by a general with well-known Girondin sympathies, reached Paris a few days later, Robespierre seized the moment. On April 10 he accused Brissot, Vergniaud, Armand Gensonné and other leading Girondin deputies of plotting, with Dumouriez and other traitors, to undermine the Revolution. He sought, unsuccessfully, their referral to the Revolutionary Tribunal.

It seems entirely possible that Robespierre acted cynically on April 10, having recognized a golden opportunity to remove from power his bitterest political rivals. In the anxious context of early April, however, it is certainly not impossible to imagine that he had convinced himself that his rivals worked in league with Dumouriez and that they had actively fomented the rebellion that now threatened to sunder the republic. (No evidence suggests this was true). Whatever his exact motives, the consequences of Robespierre's accusation are unmistakable in retrospect. His acrimonious words let loose a barrage of charges and counter-charges that spilled forth from the Convention into the streets in the ensuing days, finally leading the Convention toward an unworkable political impasse. The Girondin deputies, rallying after being thrown back on their heels, accused Robespierre's sometime-ally Marat of incitement to violence, an accusation of which he was clearly guilty, and called for and received a formal vote in the Convention on whether to try him before the Revolutionary Tribunal. The pro-radical Tribunal acquitted Marat on April 24, but not before the Paris Commune and the sections had jumped into the fray by petitioning the Convention to purge from its membership a list of twenty-two of the most vocal and determined Girondin leaders. When the Convention turned away the request, the Commune published its petition and the section leaders kept up the pressure by organizing popular action and working to radicalize the entire city.

In the first two months following the execution of Louis XVI, the government had managed to do its job reasonably well while holding in check the bitter personal hatreds that threatened to overwhelm the Convention at any moment. Over the course of April and May, however, clear battle lines were drawn. On one side stood the Paris Commune, the energized radical workers who dominated the Paris sections, and the Mountain and its allies at the Jacobin club, united in their commitment to emergency measures on both political and economic fronts (though the Mountain embraced radical economic measures only grudgingly). On the other side stood the increasingly isolated but still formally influential Girondins, united by an instinct for law and order, the principle of defending property at all costs, and a reluctance to allow Parisians to define the "general will" of the nation, even in moments of great emergency. Both sides were fully republican in their political ideologies, but neither side could countenance the continued influence of its opponents. A showdown was predetermined.

After another wave of demonstrations in May, pressures came to a head on May 18, when the Convention created a special 'Commission of Twelve' and charged it with investigating subversive activities in Paris. This clearly repressive initiative had been pushed by the Girondins, and the Commission was also packed with deputies sympathetic to their cause. (The Girondins' continuing ability to broker positive votes in the Convention may have blinded them, until it was too late, to the scale of their de-legitimation in the eyes of the Parisian populace). Over the next two weeks each side tried to intimidate the other into submission, but the contest finally concluded with an armed confrontation on June 2. François Hanriot, leader of the Parisian National Guard and ally of the most radical section leaders, surrounded the Convention and demanded the expulsion of the twenty-two targeted Girondin deputies.

Drama at the Convention

What followed was the most dramatic stare-down since Mirabeau dared royal troops to disperse the National Assembly "by the force of bayonets". As the Convention deputies recognized the seriousness of the popular military threat they now faced, they made the collective decision —supported even by many members of the Mountain— to march outside into the Tuileries courtyard to assert their independence and to try to talk the National Guardsmen down from the ledge where they were metaphorically perched. Despite initial pleasantries, Hanriot persisted in demanding the expulsion of the twenty-two suspect Girondins. The deputies refused to comply, recognizing the danger of the precedent that such expulsions would set. But Hanriot and the Guards were unwilling to take no for an answer.

> In a remarkable act of all-or-nothing resolve, they readied their weapons and prepared to fire on the deputies. In a stark reversal of the dynamic that framed the confrontation of June 1789, this time it was the men at arms who refused to relent; the elected deputies filed back into their meeting hall, defeated and aware that they were being forced onto potentially unstable extra-legal terrain. Under the watch of the National Guard, the Convention ordered the arrest of twenty-nine Girondin deputies, the balance of power within the assembly shifted in an instant, and the people of Paris successfully asserted their *de facto* superiority over the legislature. A climactic new chapter had begun.

Extreme Measures

One clear sign of the ambivalence with which the Convention carried out its purge of the Girondins was the sloppy handling of the deputies' incarceration. Many of the leading Girondins escaped in the ensuing days, fanning out to the departments, where there was considerable resentment at Paris's high-handed expulsion of duly elected representatives. The fugitive deputies worked to rally opinion against the Convention. In Normandy, one individual listened with a particularly sympathetic ear: Charlotte Corday. A convinced republican who had nevertheless been shocked by the execution of the king and the purge of the Girondins, she set off for Paris in early July. She was steeled by her determination to remove from the scene Paris's most notorious radical, Marat, and thereby carry out a corrective measure that she hoped would put the Revolution back on course. Late in the day on July 13, Corday gained access to Marat's living quarters, having intimated that she had information about new revolts being planned in the northwest. Marat, who was soaking in a medicinal bath to treat a chronic skin ailment, listened to Corday's news, evidently even taking notes as she proceeded to name names. During a moment of distraction, Corday plunged a six-inch knife into his chest, killing him instantly.

Corday's hopes —she testified under interrogation that she had taken one life in order "to save a hundred thousand"— would go unrealized. Marat's death provided the revolutionary cause a new martyr. The Montagnard painter Jacques-Louis David immediately began work on his famed portrait of the dying Marat (it would briefly hang in the Convention), and a thirst for vengeance against the Revolution's enemies would help to fuel new moves in a violent and authoritarian direction. On July 27, ten days after the Revolutionary Tribunal sent Corday to the scaffold, Robespierre joined the CPS. Danton had recently rotated off the Committee, and this July turnover is deeply symbolic. The purge of the Girondins had prompted new signs of moderation on Danton's part, as he began a slow migration away from the radical heart of the Convention. Meanwhile, Robespierre had fully reconciled himself to the *journée* of June 2, was now prepared to capitalize on the removal of the Girondin deputies from the Convention, and had come to realize that the impetus of popular anger in Paris could be harnessed to the development of robust government initiatives that could help the Revolution overcome the twin threats of war and counter-revolution. The CPS was to become the chief instrument by which Robespierre and his allies —Louis-Antoine de Saint-Just, Georges Couthon, and a handful of others on the twelve-person Committee— would seek to meld the will of the people with the unmediated power of a Convention operating in crisis mode.

Fittingly, one of the reorganized Committee's founding acts, in August, was to persuade the Convention to announce that the republican constitution recently drafted and approved by popular vote would be indefinitely suspended. The republican constitution envisioned in the aftermath of the revolution of August 10, 1792 —one whose altered *Declaration of Rights* ensured the people's right of insurrection— would need to wait to be realized in practice. It would in fact never be realized, since the perception of existential crisis demanded that the government remain "Revolutionary until the peace", as the Convention would formally announce in October. By the time peace arrived, on a temporary basis in 1797, France had passed through the crucible of the Jacobin ascendancy and had moved on to another constitution.

The year between July 1793 and July 1794, a period typically referred to as "the Reign of Terror", is easily caricatured as a time of limitless excess driven by a small number of power-mad zealots so consumed by political hatreds that they were driven to the brink of psychosis. Acts of excessive cruelty, and of exemplary punishments that seem to have served inexcusably narrow political purposes, certainly show up in the chronicle of the Revolution's most tortuous year. And many undoubtedly felt terrorized by a governing regime that successfully concentrated dictatorial powers in a single committee. But the label "the Terror" oversimplifies. By postulating the existence of a unique episode separated from the rest of the Revolutionary experience, it authorizes facile interpretation. It particularly invites the scapegoating of individuals who can be made to bear responsibility for all of the uglier features of the Revolution. This is precisely what the enemies of Robespierre set out to do, in a reflexive face-saving operation, beginning in late July of 1794. The crisis year of 1793-1794 actually emerged from dynamics inherent in the Revolution from the outset, not from the nefarious motives of individuals.

For example, the year of maximum crisis can reasonably be said to have begun with the purge of the Girondins. The purge announced the beginning of emergency government, and it set a precedent for later purges (and worse) that Robespierre and his allies executed with an unseemly degree of ruthlessness. But any evil intentions Robespierre and his allies carried toward the Girondins had been reciprocated in full for a solid year before the purge. The Girondins had schemed to have Robespierre arrested as early as July 1792, and they had been responsible for the legislation of April 1, 1793 that permitted the arrest of Convention deputies —specifically because they themselves were then taking aim at Marat. The sense of life-or-death struggle that enveloped the deputies of the Mountain and the Girondins in 1793 had been generated through conflicts that reflected the central tensions coursing through the Revolution since 1789 —conflicts arising from the king's treachery, the disturbing growth of counter-revolutionary sentiment and activity, the challenge of mitigating intermittent economic misery, and the pressures exerted both by foreign adversaries and a frustrated populace willing to take the law into its own hands.

All of these festering conflicts were exacerbated by problems specific to the summer of 1793: counter-revolution triumphant in the Vendée, localized rebellions in other important cities such as Lyon, Marseille, Nîmes, and Bordeaux, and coalition armies on the march in the north. In light of these overlapping crises, which together constituted a grave and unprecedented threat to the Revolution's viability, the Convention granted the Committee of

Public Safety extraordinary powers. It also supported the Committee's use of those powers with few reservations before the summer of 1794. Most of the measures that made up what historians refer to as "the Terror" sprang naturally from the anxieties that beset the Convention in the summer of 1793.

The first priority remained the war effort, and August saw a doubling down of the Convention's determination to raise the forces necessary to repel foreign enemies. On August 14 the CPS gained the services of Lazare Carnot, a former engineer from the royal army whose bureaucratic talent and attention to detail would eventually earn him the sobriquet "the organizer of victory". At Carnot's urging, the CPS had the Convention declare a *levée en masse* (mass levy of recruits). This levy raised at least half a million men by early 1794, but the recruitment of new soldiers was only one part of an integrated plan to build a newly effective war machine. The Convention expropriated buildings owned by *émigrés* and the church and converted them into foundries or barracks. Horses and draught animals were requisitioned across the country. Artisans and laborers had to make themselves available for the manufacturing of guns and ammunition, and the Convention appropriated funds to pay for their services. Women would serve in hospitals and prepare new uniforms and tents. New battalions of soldiers would organize themselves under a banner that read "The French People Risen Against Tyrants". By early 1794, these redoubled efforts began to pay dividends, as French armies once again moved onto the offensive and foretold the string of astounding military successes that stretched from 1796 to 1807.

In the Revolution's fight for survival in 1793, however, the war effort represented one side of a coin stamped also by the threat of internal dissent. The story of the gradual pacification of the rebellious regions beyond Paris in the late summer and fall of 1793 contained scenes of horror that make any dispassionate student of the Revolution recoil. Some of the worst atrocities took place in and around the Vendée, south of Brittany, where pitiless republican generals slaughtered men, women, and children indiscriminately. Whole villages disappeared in the carnage. A particularly zealous representative-on-mission, Jean-Baptiste Carrier, loaded captives on boats, bound their hands and feet, and then set them afloat in the Loire river where they were sent to watery deaths. These so-called *noyades* (execution by drowning) claimed several thousand victims. Toward the end of the repressive operations in the Vendée, the CPS's appointed general Louis Marie Turreau ordered soldiers to follow a scorched earth policy to eliminate any remaining rebels. They marched across the landscape in "infernal columns", putting everything to the torch and executing every last suspect, regardless of age or gender. In all, republican forces are estimated to have killed over 100,000 people in the Vendée.

Nor was the Vendée alone in absorbing the fury of the Convention's angry representatives-on-mission. At Toulon, an important port city on the Mediterranean that had made the cardinal error of surrendering to the British navy in August 1793, the conquering republican army (featuring Napoleon Bonaparte in a newly significant role) effectively turned captive citizens over to local Jacobins who had remained loyal to the Republic; they carried out mass executions, and as many as one thousand Toulonnais died in the wave of retribution that rolled across the city in December 1793. In that same month, rebels in the country's second-largest city of Lyon, which had been retaken by republican armies after a months-long siege, faced a similarly brutal fate. Hundreds were mowed down by cannon fire, with many hundreds more executed by firing squad (in *fusillades*, death by gun fire) between December and February. Vengeful violence on a smaller scale also occurred in Caen, Bordeaux, and Marseille in late 1793 and early 1794.

These measures, ordered or endorsed after the fact by the CPS and carried out by soldiers and local officials blinded by their thirst for vengeance, cannot be excused through any normal lens of judgment. Yet civil wars have always been marked by episodes of vindictive rage and exceptional cruelty. During France's Wars of Religion in the sixteenth century, for example, thousands of Protestants, most of them unarmed, were slaughtered during the Saint Bartholomew's Day massacre of 1572; Catholics suffered equally brutal reprisals for years to come. In the American Civil War in 1864, meanwhile, on a march through Virginia's Shenandoah Valley, the Union general Philip Sheridan deployed a tactic that approximated the "infernal columns". Having been instructed to leave the region barren, he had his soldiers burn everything of value over a one hundred-mile radius —crops, meadows, homes, businesses— leaving thousands of civilians without food and shelter. When locked in a life or death struggle seemingly provoked or exacerbated by a betrayal from within, the push for victory gains reinforcement from a will to punish and a desire to create examples that will serve as a deterrent. The path from existential fear to frenzied vengeance is short and direct.

Existential fears, within the body of the Convention, were both heightened and given ideological ballast by the claims of the people of Paris. Not even the most radical members of the Mountain condoned the wanton destruction of property or uncontrolled crowd violence —Marat himself had denounced the Parisian food riots of February 1793, for example— but an inclination to legitimize and respond to the people's anger, and to endorse their purposeful political action, had been a key dividing line separating the disapproving Girondins from their more radical counterparts during the first nine months of the Republic. It is not surprising, then, that after the purge of June 2, the Convention showed a new willingness to accede to popular demands, on both the political and economic fronts. From the point of view of the radicalized members of the sections, the clubs, and the Commune, the current political and economic emergencies were indistinguishable. The imperative to provision the capital with food required politically repressive measures against hoarders, price gougers, and speculators. "Famine", as one citizen announced at a section meeting in late July, "is one of the secrets tyrants use to subjugate peoples", and only pro-active measures could prevent Europe's rulers and their accomplices from starving the Revolution into submission.

Pressure to implement emergency measures that would simultaneously secure the food supply and eliminate counter-revolutionaries built steadily throughout summer and fall 1793, and the Convention responded. Already on June 4, the deputies decreed the creation of "revolutionary armies" —bands of roving patriots authorized to use rough tactics to convert "political sinners", punish hoarders, and root out counter-revolutionary elements in every community. In August, also partly in response to popular pressure, the Convention's Committee on Legislation began working on a "Law of Suspects" that would specify whose activities could be rightly classified as suspect and therefore susceptible to the punishment of detention or expulsion. The law would reactivate and energize local surveillance committees throughout the next year. The mass levy of military recruits was also announced in late August.

All of these measures, and others, were formalized in the wake of another dramatic *journée* on September 5, 1793. Just days after Paris had received the alarming news of Toulon's capitulation to the British, representatives from the sections, the clubs, and the Commune —a cross-section of Parisian *sans-culottes*— stormed into the Convention and demanded stern measures and prompt action from a body perceived as dithering in the face of growing threats. Historians often make this event the official birthdate of the "reign of Terror", because in the heat of the confrontation one of the protestors called on the deputies "to make terror the order of the day". The Convention never made any such announcement, however, and there is little to suggest that the legislative initiatives announced that day or elaborated in the weeks after were viewed as making up a new and fully integrated system of governance. Instead, they were discrete measures taken to address specific problems or looming emergencies, and the duration and terms of implementation for each of these measures remained subject to the discretion of the CPS and the Convention.

The CPS indeed adjusted its emergency measures over time. The Convention adopted a "Law of the General Maximum" in late September 1793, imposing price controls on foodstuffs and other critical supplies. But the law never applied as generally or as severely as Parisian activists would have preferred, and the CPS developed the habit of looking the other way when violations of the law resulted not from treachery or greed but from obvious market shortages. Similarly, in December 1793 the Convention passed a law that reined in the representatives on mission, whose revolutionary zeal had led in numerous cases to unjust imprisonments, the destruction of churches, and even a "de-Christianizing" campaign that threatened to alienate otherwise sympathetic citizens in the hinterlands. In the spring of 1794 the Convention dismantled the "revolutionary armies" for similar reasons. Even extreme measures adopted in the context of an ongoing emergency were not deliberately intended to promote excess.

Revolutionary Purity

One message the CPS was consistently determined to convey, however, was that the removal of the Girondin deputies had also removed any reluctance to move against the Revolution's enemies. Such reticence had spelled trouble for the National Assembly in the wake of the king's flight, for the Legislative Assembly in the lead-up to the republican revolution, and for the Convention itself in April-May, 1793 in the wake of Dumouriez's defection and the food shortages allegedly caused by hoarders. One might compare the collective psyche of the Revolution's most ardent supporters in 1793 to victims of serial abuse who are moved to become crusaders for the cause of prevention. The experience of betrayal had so colored the entire history of the Revolution that the post-purge Convention, and the Committee of Public Safety that served as its emergency instrument, pursued "the last enemy of liberty" with unprecedented vigor. As Saint-Just framed it in an October speech, the government would now punish "not only the traitors, but even those who are indifferent". An obsessive desire to purify the political ground, and to cleanse the republic of those who had betrayed it or who might betray it in the future, meant that the CPS would execute a furious civil war in the legal arena —trying, convicting, and guillotining the politically dangerous as well as the ghosts of betrayals past.

The political trials that marked the period from October 1793 through July 1794, and which feature so prominently in most accounts of the French Revolution, thus served two explicable if not entirely defensible purposes. Both to show the people that the government was at last fully revolutionary and to secure the Revolution's survival against the many internal enemies that had worked or would work to overthrow it, the CPS carried out an uncompromising judicial war against those it considered guilty of betrayal. As in most fratricidal conflicts, the harshest treatment was meted out to those closest to the center of action and thus most resented for their treachery: government officials. In early October 1793, just two weeks after the formal passage of the

Law of Suspects, the former queen was at last sent to the Revolutionary Tribunal, where she was forced to listen to absurd accusations of her alleged sexual deviancy in addition to the damning, and true, charge that she had long acted as an Austrian agent. Her conviction foreordained, Marie-Antoinette went to a dignified death on October 16, so self-possessed on the scaffold that she apologized to her executioner for stepping on his toes.

The long-anticipated elimination of the queen opened the floodgates in the fall of 1793. The former Girondin deputies, including those who had been recaptured in the course of the summer, were tried at the end of October. One, Charles Dufriche-Valazé, stabbed himself to death on the floor of the Revolutionary Tribunal as his guilty verdict was read aloud; Brissot and the rest of the famed twenty-two faced the scaffold bravely, joyously singing the *Marseillaise* as they trundled toward their fate. The Duc d'Orléans, a cousin to Louis XVI who had voted for his execution and who had taken on the moniker Philippe Egalité in 1792, was deemed guilty by association with Girondins and took his turn at the scaffold in early November. Other leading lights from earlier episodes of the Revolution —the ex-Feuillant Antoine Barnave, two former Parisian mayors, Jérôme Pétion and Jean-Sylvain Bailly (of Champ de Mars infamy), the *salonnière* Madame Roland, the playwright Olympe de Gouges— likewise fell under the blade of the guillotine, their crimes having been their earlier advocacy for moderation. As Saint-Just had explained, "those who are indifferent", particularly those who enjoyed power or influence, would now suffer the Revolution's wrath.

From late November until the following July, the Revolutionary Tribunal and its satellites in the provinces also dispatched many living symbols of the *Ancien Régime*. François de L'Averdy, a controller-general who had lifted restrictions on the market in grains in 1764, leading to severe bread shortages, was pulled out of obscurity and charged with plotting to cause famine while in office. Author of a past betrayal, he was guillotined on November 24, 1793. One of his contemporaries, Louis XV's last mistress, Jeanne Bécu, comtesse du Barry, was accused of providing financial support to *émigrés* and counter-revolutionaries. She was executed in early December.

Killing the Symbols of the Ancien Régime

Late December saw the arrest of Lamoignon de Malesherbes, magistrate in a former tax court and a royal censor who had provided sympathy and protection to philosophes. Author of an influential 1775 treatise that had denounced the "despotism" of the king's administrators, his chief crime in 1793 was the vigorous legal defense he provided the king at the time of his trial. The *parlementaire* Duval d'Eprémesnil, remembered for his controversial

> championing of the "forms of 1614" in 1788, spent time with Malesherbes in prison as he awaited his own execution. The same was true of the noted chemist and tax farmer Antoine Lavoisier, member of the exalted but now suppressed Academy of Sciences. Nicolas de Caritat, marquis de Condorcet, was arguably the last of the great Enlightenment philosophes. His *Sketch for a Historical Picture of the Progress of the Human Spirit*, written in the last months of his life, encapsulated better than any other text the faith in social progress that had helped to inspire and guide the early stages of the Revolution. Condorcet was nevertheless tainted by his association with the Girondins, and he lived his last weeks on the run from the authorities. By May 1794, all four of these luminaries from a lost world were dead —Condorcet by suicide in a jail cell and the others by guillotine.

By the spring of 1794, the government's propensity to see all political challenges through the lens of civil war, as derived from a Manichean struggle between darkness and light, reached new levels of intensity and finally pushed the CPS toward instability. In the summer and fall of 1793, the widely relished prospect of punishing prominent enemies —Marat's assassin, a hated royal mistress, an even more hated queen, the conspiring Girondins, to say nothing of the rebels in the Vendée— allowed the post-purge Convention and its machinery of repression to operate in a state of uneasy equilibrium. By the spring, however, consensus proved elusive. Some, particularly the radical *sans-culottes* and their journalistic spokespersons, had been cheered by the bloodletting of the fall and called for even more thorough-going purgative measures. By March, a few were openly calling for insurrection against the purported "moderates" in the Convention. These "ultra" revolutionaries, as they were called, were countered by an *ad hoc* coalition, which included leading Convention deputies Danton and Desmoulins, who believed the time had come for the CPS to relax its tight grip over French society and move toward the normalization of government protocols. Robespierre and other members of the CPS saw both this "Indulgent" faction and the audacious "ultras" as threats not only to the authority of the Convention, and to its all-powerful Committee, but to the progress that had been made against the Revolution's enemies in the previous eight months. Over several weeks in March-April, the CPS moved against both perceived threats.

The Parisian radicals, and the brand of populism to which they gave voice, went first. An early sign of the CPS's willingness to crack down even on the radicals who provided their firmest base of support had come in November 1793, when the Convention banned the Society of Revolutionary Republican Women for its noisy demonstrations and its tendency to denounce the Convention for its moderation. The journalist Jacques Hébert, a star at the Cordeliers Club and a hero to working people in Paris, echoed their language in early March, thus triggering among Robespierre and his allies a fear that even some *sans-culottes* were now working with foreigners and counter-revolutionaries to undermine the legitimacy of Revolutionary government. By the middle of the month, Hébert and about fifteen of his allies and associates had been arrested, charged with plotting against the Convention, and placed on trial. They made their way to the guillotine on March 24.

Only a week later, the CPS made plans for a symmetrical purge that would take out Danton, Desmoulins, and several other "moderate" deputies in the Convention. Danton had long been suspected, with reason, of engaging in graft. But now he and his Indulgent allies were accused of enabling all the Revolution's most vexing problems: inflation, food shortages, and rebellion. Saint-Just, in a speech on the floor of the Convention the morning after his arrest, even accused Danton of being an "aristocrat" —an incongruous allegation to throw at the man who, as minister of justice in August of 1792, authorized the "domiciliary visits" that had helped pave the way toward the September prison massacres. Whether the members of the CPS who cooked up these allegations believed them seems doubtful. But the motor that had driven the work of the Committee since its reconstitution in the previous July had been its instinct to see in every indicator of personal disloyalty to the Revolution, as defined by the work of the CPS itself, proof of the presence of a darkened counter-revolutionary heart. Operating on that premise, and convinced that the Revolution's survival depended on their own survival, the members of the CPS would find it natural to blend all the characteristics of the "counter-revolutionary" on one large palette, and to apply the various colors indiscriminately to those who stood accused of yet another betrayal. Danton, despite a heroic courtroom performance in his own defense, was convicted. He and Desmoulins, with several of their allies, went to the guillotine on April 5, 1794, providing startling evidence for Vergniaud's earlier aphorism that "the Revolution is devouring its own".

The immediate effect of the staggering moves against Hébert and Danton in March and April was to further centralize power in the CPS. The committee soon took on new policing powers of its own, eroding the authority of one of its sister committees. The Convention also authorized a judicial streamlining of cases involving counter-revolutionary activity in the departments outside Paris; with few exceptions, these would now be judged in the capital. In the wake of the execution of its most charismatic leaders, even the Cordeliers Club shuttered, leaving the Jacobins unrivaled as the semi-official articulators of Revolutionary principles.

The executions of the Hébertists and Dantonists nevertheless altered the political dynamics of the Revolution in ways that would prove conclusive.

Robespierre and his colleagues were given free rein in the two months after the purge of Danton, but this was largely because other members of the Convention, initially in shock, only gradually came to terms with a new realization: the sudden elimination of figures as heroic as Danton and as popular as Hébert meant that no one could feel safe. That reality received reinforcement on June 10, when the CPS pushed through a new law (the law of 22 Prairial, according to the naturalistic terms of the new republican calendar) that refashioned the Revolutionary Tribunal as an instrument of "prompt, severe, inflexible justice", as Robespierre had put it earlier in the year in a speech on the use of terror as a political tactic. According to the new law, which also shrank the size of the Tribunal to increase efficiency, those accused of treason could bring no witnesses for the defense, and jurors would focus on eliminating the "enemies of the people". The criteria to qualify as an enemy were expansive. The category included those who "sought to inspire discouragement", who "disseminated false news", who "sought to disparage or dissolve the National Convention", as well as those who "sought to mislead opinion". It is no coincidence that roughly half the 2,600 Parisians executed by the Revolutionary Tribunal between its creation in April 1793 and late July 1794 were convicted after 22 Prairial.

This move toward greater severity in the punishment of internal enemies coincided, ironically, with a series of military triumphs against France's external enemies —including most prominently the June 26 battle of Fleurus in the Austrian Netherlands, the great turning point in France's war against the first coalition. With the Vendée also at least temporarily pacified, the ostensible rationale for the stringent measures advocated by the CPS slowly and then suddenly dissipated. When Saint-Just and Couthon gave speeches, in late July, intimating that a new purge of the Convention might be in the offing, they increased the paranoia of several configurations of the assembly's deputies who became desperate to save themselves. Because Robespierre, Saint-Just and Couthon had become the face of the CPS, they became the targets of the terrorized deputies. An inflammatory speech by Robespierre delivered on the floor of the convention on July 26, in which he broadcast vague accusations of treason against a dozen or more deputies —he promised to "punish the traitors…[and] to purify the CPS itself"— finally provoked a response. Long known as the "Incorruptible", Robespierre seems to have internalized this image of himself as the inerrant lodestar of republican patriotism. But by defining the circle of purity so narrowly, effectively to include only himself and his two most loyal partners, he had presented his colleagues a do-or-die choice.

> ## Robespierre's Fall
>
> The fall came swiftly, though not without considerable drama. Several deputies jumped to their feet to challenge Robespierre's "slanders". Stunned by the show of defiance, he backpedaled as the meeting was officially adjourned. He rushed to the Jacobin club and rallied some support, but his opponents worked through the night to strategize over the proceedings for the coming day's Convention meeting. As Saint-Just took the floor on July 27 (9 Thermidor in the republican calendar), a series of deputies sowed chaos in the Convention by hurling objections on the basis of process. When Robespierre moved to assist Saint-Just, multiple deputies shouted "down with the tyrant!" Others evoked Danton and accused Robespierre of having assassinated a model patriot. Then, with the piercing suddenness of a cannon shot, several other deputies called for the arrest of the Incorruptible himself. He, Saint-Just, Couthon, and several lesser lights were immediately detained by the Convention's committee in charge of policing.

The captives managed to escape later that night. They found refuge in the offices of the Paris Commune at City Hall. There they hoped the radicals of the sections and the Paris National Guard, still under the direction of Hanriot, would come to their rescue.

But popular enthusiasm for the men who betrayed Hébert had long since waned, and more troops opted to support the Convention and the rule of law than the faltering cause of Robespierre. In the early hours of July 28, the forces of the Convention finally burst in and overwhelmed the fugitive prisoners, who struggled to the last. Their mutilated but still palpitating bodies —Robespierre had been shot in the jaw, his brother suffered a broken leg, Couthon had fallen down a marble staircase— were dragged to the guillotine in the afternoon of July 28. Hanriot, former scourge of the Girondins, went down with them.

Assessments After 9 Thermidor

When the elected deputies of the Three Estates convened at Versailles in May 1789, no one knew where or how their unprecedented political journey would end. In July of that year, a British diplomat helpfully reported to his superiors in London, after the fall of the Bastille and the king's affirmation of the legitimacy of the National Assembly, that "the Revolution in the French Constitution and Government may now, I think, be looked upon as completed". This proved premature. Roughly two years later, the representative Isaac-René-Guy Le Chapelier would hail the completion of the Constitution of 1791 as putting an end to a "time of destruction". Noting that "no abuses remain to be abolished", he affirmed with confidence that "everyone wants the Revolution to be ended". Others disagreed. Vergniaud, in the midst of the Girondins' fruitless efforts to curb popular radicalism in March 1793, insisted on the floor of the Convention that the Revolution had reached its end "the instant that France was constituted as a republic". One year later, in that same assembly, an indignant Saint-Just sought to defame Danton by ascribing to him the suspect belief that "the Revolution is over". And a little more than five years later, Napoleon Bonaparte, on the day after the coup of November 9, 1799 that ended the republic and made him First Consul, still found it necessary to decree: "Citizens, the Revolution is over".

For the participants in the great event, ending the French Revolution proved to be a daunting challenge. For students of the Revolution, however, the coup against the *de facto* leaders of the CPS on July 27, 1794 constitutes a sharp dividing line and serves as the most logical ending point for an exploration of the essence of the French Revolution. To be sure, the republic would survive until 1799, and some of the prominent individuals from earlier phases of the Revolution —the *abbé* Sieyès, Henri Grégoire, Carnot— crossed the divide of Thermidor and made important contributions to later events.

The nature of the republic that survived into the late 1790s was far different, however, from that first envisioned in August 1792. Those who vanquished the king at the Tuileries and who founded the First

Republic on September 22, 1792 believed at least implicitly in the inherent authority of a mobilized populace. Popular activism had fueled the Revolution from its first days, and the *Declaration of Rights* of 1793 had referred to insurrection as "the most sacred of rights and the most indispensable of duties" whenever the government "violates the rights of the people". In the year that followed the execution of Robespierre and company, however, the Convention and France's broader political culture moved steadily in the opposite direction. As the tools of emergency government were slowly dismantled, many came to be persuaded that the multiple tragedies of the Revolution's first five years had derived from the political elite's excessive deference toward the people's authority.

The newly configured republic that began to take shape by the end of 1794 would favor the propertied classes and would act with severity toward all manifestations of popular unrest. François Boissy d'Anglas, one of the architects of the refashioned republic, captured the new attitude in 1795. "We must be governed by the best", he announced to a Convention that was then contemplating further revisions to the republican constitution. "The best are those who are best educated and most interested in the maintenance of the laws". With very few exceptions, he continued, "you find such men only among those who, owning a piece of property, are devoted to the country that contains it, to the laws that protect it, to the tranquility that maintains it". The new constitution that the Convention approved in August 1795 installed a system of voting that secured disproportionate power for the wealthy, and it expressly forbade collective political action outside of electoral assemblies. No political clubs were allowed, no collective petitions could be submitted to the legislature, and even "unarmed gathering[s]" of citizens were to be dispersed, if necessary, "by the deployment of armed force". The government had grown mistrustful of the unofficial organs of democracy.

8. Statue of Napoleon Bonaparte, *Les Invalides*, Paris, France.

Significantly, the decision to draft and approve this new, more restrictive and less populist, constitution had been triggered by recent popular affronts to the Convention's authority. The winter of 1795 was among the coldest on record, and it combined with a weak harvest from the previous autumn to inflict great misery on ordinary people throughout France. The remnants of the Parisian *sans-culottes* movement had been chanting "bread and the constitution of 1793" throughout the winter, and on April 1 an impromptu gathering of demonstrators marched into the meeting hall of the Convention and demanded action. They extracted only vague promises, but they clarified in the minds of the increasingly moderate Convention deputies the strategy that would need to be pursued finally to restore order to the Revolution. The deputies appointed a committee to revise the constitution. A second unruly crowd action on May 20 —leading to the decapitation of one deputy and the waving of his head before the face of a stricken Boissy d'Anglas— sealed the fate of the remaining radicals within the Convention (six more were guillotined) and led to harshly repressive measures against the Paris sections. Activists in these former motors of Parisian radicalism were forced to turn over their weapons.

July 27, 1794 thus constitutes a watershed. To that point in the Revolution the power of popular activism had regularly propelled events; in the wake of the coup against the CPS, the people were systematically disempowered. One of the great questions that had haunted the Revolution since the taking of the Bastille —when and to what extent should the extra-legal actions of "the people" count as legitimate?— had been definitively answered. It is important to note that this answer came not immediately after Robespierre's fall, but only over the course of months, as the Convention and the rest of the country gradually settled on the meaning of the events that had ensued from the purge of the Girondins. The deputies who took down Robespierre, Saint-Just, and Couthon should not be misconstrued as the "principled" actors in this conflict, the ones who sought only to restore greater humanity to the operations of government. Several had committed atrocities of their own, and many deputies had assumed that severe measures would remain in place after Robespierre's ouster. Their first and main priority in sidelining the Incorruptible was to save their own skins. All members of the Convention had shown a capacity to be indifferent to viciousness, but Robespierre was likely the most scrupulous of the whole lot —though he was scrupulous in observance of an arguably immoral code. He resorted to violent measures less out of self-interest than out of his conviction that, in the ongoing civil war of good versus evil, the salvation of the republic required the violence that he (and not only he) continued to endorse or direct to the end.

Still, in the months after Robespierre's death many people, including some of his partners in terror, saw advantage in stigmatizing him as the principal author of a cruel episode that had deviated from the Revolution's original principles. Implicated in this contrived backlash against Robespierrism (and also Jacobinism) was the expectation that the authority of the people should be heeded in times of political emergency —an expectation Robespierre carried with him for the entirety of the Revolution, up to his break with Hébert. But popular activism cannot really be blamed for the failures of the Revolution. Consider the fate of the "Directory" —a shorthand that refers to the entire republican government of the second half of the 1790s, though the term technically applies only to the five-person executive panel crafted for this new government.

As noted, the designers of the constitution of 1795 expressly undercut popular political activism in France. There would be no further Parisian uprisings or demonstrations after 1795, and the government used ruthless tactics to quell unrest and put down regional rebellions in the late 1790s. The state more or less successfully enforced the "tranquility" Boissy d'Anglas had called for in his address to the Convention in 1795. Despite this changed dynamic, the Directory did not survive. It failed because of its inability to negotiate the "politics of the balance beam", that is, its need to hold at bay both the resurgent royalist forces that threatened to undo the republic and the never entirely extinguished radicals who pined for a return to the policies and constitution of 1793. After annulling the results of two consecutive national elections in 1797 and 1798 —because of the election of too many "extremists", first from the right and then from the left— the Directory sank into dysfunctionality. Facing new military threats from the crowned heads of Europe in 1799, the Directors invited the charismatic general Napoleon Bonaparte to stage a military coup that sounded the death knell of the First Republic.

The period 1794-1799, then, was also racked by a mutual, and ultimately fatal, distrust between left and right —even though popular agitation on the streets of Paris had been removed from the political equation. The year of Robespierre's ascendancy therefore should not be bracketed off from the supposedly more "liberal" periods that preceded and followed it. In many ways, the year of terror marked the culmination of the Revolution's potential and its ideals. The year saw the drafting of France's most egalitarian and democratic constitution before the twentieth century. After its commissioner in Saint-Domingue liberated the slaves of that colony for strategic military purposes in 1793, the National Convention followed up in February 1794 by decreeing "that all men, without distinction of color, residing in the colonies are French citizens and will enjoy all the rights assured by the constitution". (Napoleon would later rescind this emancipatory decree). The post-purge Convention also demonstrated to the world that a democratically elected government could marshal the will and the resources not only to repel foreign invasion but to embark on the conquest of Europe. Revolutionary government, at the height of existential emergency, proved efficacious.

The year 1793-1794 also saw horrible bloodletting and uncontrolled political passions. More than 16,000 people, all across the country, were sentenced to death by revolutionary tribunals in the year that followed the ouster of the Girondins, and the total death toll for Year II of the republic, counting not only political executions but fatalities in the civil war that raged in the Vendée and intermittently in other regions, probably topped a quarter million. Atrocious cruelty was a dominant strain in the political culture of France between July 1793 and July 1794.

The regrettable and essential ugliness of 1793-1794 nevertheless bore the traces of all the previous conflicts that had defined the French Revolution since June 1789. Those conflicts arose from the clash of old and new, from the competing interests of those who benefited or saw value in the status quo, on the one hand, and those who pursued the promise of transformative change, on the other hand. Such conflicts symbolize the messiness of the process of revolution itself. Exacerbating those conflicts in the French case, however, was a series of betrayals or perceived betrayals that made suspicion a permanent condition of revolutionary life. Louis XVI stood out as the prime offender on this score, but other one-time heroes had also been exposed as untrustworthy: Mirabeau, Lafayette, Bailly, Barnave, Dumouriez, even Necker. This list of luminaries leaves aside the imaginary "brigands" of the summer of 1789, the "secret" hoarders, the National Assembly's craven decision to protect a traitorous king in 1791, the threats from *émigrés* and priests, and the personalized and mutually repellent distrust that drove apart the Girondins and the radicals of the Mountain. Brissot had once dreamed of exposing all plots in 1792, but the "great doses of poison" he evoked had penetrated to the suspicious heart of the Revolution. The rhythms of the Revolution had been dictated by betrayal and the anticipation of further betrayals; the violent popular energies that Robespierre had sought to utilize and contain all flowed from such betrayals.

The emergency measures the Convention began to adopt even before the expulsion of the Girondins, and which it sought to reinforce throughout the fall of 1793 —the general activation of surveillance committees, the establishment of the Revolutionary Tribunal, the passage of a Law of Suspects, the laws against hoarders, the formation of roving "revolutionary armies" in perpetual search of counter-revolutionaries— represented not only a response to dangerous circumstances, as some have suggested by way of exculpatory explanation for the carnage of Year II. Those emergency measures were also responses to circumstances whose meaning had been determined by legacies of betrayal. They were symptoms of a kind of psychological trauma imposed by the experience of the Revolution itself. Section leaders had demanded a new "reign of truth" on the eve of the republican Revolution of August 10. The encompassing tragedy of the French Revolution is that an entrenched and widely shared conviction that the full truth remained forever veiled or disguised contaminated the work of successive waves of revolutionary actors. A hard-earned and pervasive bitterness prevented the construction of a unified republic capable of trust and forgiveness.

The soil in which the French Revolution took root proved infertile. Despite passionate and mostly well-intentioned efforts, the revolutionaries failed to bring to fruition the regenerated and humanitarian polity they visualized in successive stages between 1789 and 1794. Nevertheless, the principles and ideals they articulated and pursued in those years outlived their originators and spread far beyond the place of their birth. The ideals of personal liberty, universal human rights, economic equity and the people's right to subsistence, national self-determination, universal education, participatory democracy, and the accountability of the governors before the governed all survived the tumultuous revolutionary decade. They infused and inspired revolutionary movements across the globe in the nineteenth and twentieth centuries. The French Revolution devoured its own to a deplorable degree, but its greatest legacy is that it provided "great doses" of optimism, idealism, and liberating energy to all who suffered injustice in the generations after Napoleon saw fit to declare that "the Revolution is over".

Further reading

Most quoted materials come either from Keith Michael Baker, ed., *The Old Regime and the French Revolution* (Cambridge, 1987), or the website for George Mason University's invaluable project, *Liberté, Egalité, Fraternité: Exploring the French Revolution* (*http://chnm.gmu.edu/revolution/*).

The literature on the French Revolution is vast, and this list of recommended readings is highly selective. I include mainly those books and articles on which I leaned heavily for help in conceiving and framing my discussions of many of the events described in this *Quick Immersion*:

David Andress, *The Terror: The merciless war for freedom in revolutionary France* (New York, 2005).

--, ed., *The Oxford Handbook of the French Revolution* (Oxford, 2015).

Marc Belissa and Yannick Bosc, *Robespierre: La fabrication d'un mythe* (Paris, 2013).

Michel Biard et Hervé Leuwers, eds., *Visages de la Terreur* (Paris, 2014).

Léonard Burnand, *Les Pamphlets contre Necker: médias et imaginaire politique au XVIIIe siècle* (Paris, 2009).

Peter R. Campbell, Thomas E. Kaiser, Marisa Linton, eds., *Conspiracy in the French Revolution* (Manchester, 2007).

Clarke Garrett, "The Myth of the Counterrevolution in 1789", *French Historical Studies* 18 (1994): 784-800.

Jacques Godechot, *The Taking of the Bastille. July 14, 1789*, trans. Jean Stewart (New York, 1970).

Vivian Gruder, *The Notables and the Nation: the political schooling of the French* (Cambridge, Mass., 2007).

Patrice Guennifey, *La Politique de la Terreur: essai sur la violence révolutionnaire, 1789-1794* (Paris, 2000).

Colin Jones, *The Great Nation: France from Louis XIV to Napoleon* (New York, 2002).

Annie Jourdan, *Nouvelle Histoire de la Révolution* (Paris, 2018).

Marisa Linton, *Choosing Terror: virtue, friendship, and authenticity in the French Revolution* (Oxford, 2015).

Jean-Clément Martin, "Révolution Française et 'Violence Totale'", *Revue d'Histoire Moderne et Contemporaine* 66 (2019): 108-114.

--, *Violence et Révolution: Essai sur la naissance d'un mythe national* (Paris, 2006).

Raphaël Matta-Duvignau, *Gouverner, Administrer Révolutionnairement: le comité de Salut public (6 avril 1793 – 4 brumaire an IV)* (Paris, 2013).

Jeremy D. Popkin, *You Are All Free: The Haitian revolution and the abolition of slavery* (Cambridge, 2010).

Munro Price, "Mirabeau and the Court: Some New Evidence", *French Historical Studies* 29 (2006): 37-75.

Anne Roulland-Boulestreau, *Les Colonnes Infernales: violences et guerre civile en Vendée militaire (1794-1795)* (Paris, 2015).

William H. Sewell, Jr., *A Rhetoric of Bourgeois Revolution: The Abbé Sieyes and* What is the Third Estate? (Durham, N. C., 1994).

--, "Historical Events as Transformations of Structures: Inventing Revolution at the Bastille", *Theory and Society* 25 (1996): 841-881.

Barry Shapiro, *Traumatic Politics: the deputies and the king in the early French Revolution* (University Park, Penn., 2009).

Gilbert Shapiro and John Markoff, *Revolutionary Demands: A content analysis of the* cahiers de doléances *of 1789* (Stanford, 1998).

Jay M. Smith, ed., *The French Nobility in the Eighteenth Century: Reassessments and New Approaches* (University Park, Penn., 2006).

Timothy Tackett, *Becoming a Revolutionary: The deputies of the French national assembly and the emergence of a revolutionary culture (1789-1790)* (Princeton, 1996).

--, *The Coming of the Terror in the French Revolution* (Cambridge, Mass., 2015).

--, *When the King Took Flight* (Cambridge, Mass., 2003).

Sophie Wahnich, *In Defence of the Terror: liberty or death in the French Revolution*, trans. David Fernbach (London, 2012).

A Quick Immersion series

1. **De-Extinctions,** Carles Lalueza-Fox
2. **Populisms,** Carlos de la Torre
3. **Happiness,** Amitava Krishna Dutt and Benjamin Radcliff
4. **The Science of Cooking,** Claudi Mans
5. **Aristotle,** C.D.C. Reeve
6. **Jewish Culture,** Jess Olson
7. **Fascism,** Roger Griffin
8. **Nonviolence,** Andrew Fiala
9. **The French Revolution,** Jay M. Smith

For more information visit our web site
www.quickimmersions.com

www.ingramcontent.com/pod-product-compliance
Lightning Source LLC
Chambersburg PA
CBHW070640050426
42451CB00008B/231